Rural Humor

Slice of Americana...

(Life of a Tractor Salesman)

Rural Humor
Slice of Americana...
(Life of a Tractor Salesman)

by
Kevin Schmidt
cheapcountryhick@aol.com

CCB Publishing
British Columbia, Canada

Rural Humor:
Slice of Americana... (Life of a Tractor Salesman)

Copyright ©2016 by Kevin Schmidt
ISBN-13 978-1-77143-282-5
Second Edition

Library and Archives Canada Cataloguing in Publication
Schmidt, Kevin, 1959-, author
Rural humor : slice of Americana... (life of a tractor salesman)
/ by Kevin Schmidt. -- Second edition.
Issued in print and electronic formats.
ISBN 978-1-77143-282-5 (pbk.).--ISBN 978-1-77143-283-2(pdf)
Additional cataloguing data available from Library and Archives Canada

Originally published under the title *Best Rural Humor Book, Period. Slice of Americana* by Xlibris Corporation in 2010 (hard cover, paperback, e-book).

All images contained herein are used with permission or are the property of Kevin Schmidt.

Extreme care has been taken by the author to ensure that all information presented in this book is accurate and up to date at the time of publishing. Neither the author nor the publisher can be held responsible for any errors or omissions. Additionally, neither is any liability assumed for damages resulting from the use of the information contained herein.

All rights reserved. No part of this publication may be reproduced, stored in a retrieval system or transmitted in any form or by any means, electronic, mechanical, photocopying, recording or otherwise without the express written permission of the author, except in the case of excerpts used in brief reviews or publications.

Publisher: CCB Publishing
             British Columbia, Canada
             www.ccbpublishing.com

Contents

About the Author 7

Acknowledgments 11

Chapter 1
    Company Trips (and Personal Trips) 13
    Company Meetings 13
    Eating Places (very many over the years; just look at me) 13

Chapter 2
    True Stories 44
    Words of Wisdom, Quotes and Sayings
    (I heard mostly from farmers) 44

Chapter 3
    Rural Humor Funny Stories About Rural America
    (some true, some partially true, some just pure *bull*! 68

Chapter 4
    Cheap Country Hick (take the test!) 111

Closing Comments (finally!) 115

About the Author

I was born September 26, 1959, in Wyandot Memorial Hospital to Virginia and Richard Schmidt. I have lived in Lovell, Ohio my entire life (other than five years when I was first married). It took me a while to get my wife to move out in the sticks from the big city of Upper Sandusky (pop. 6,000). Our family came here and settled from Germany in the 1850's in Lovell, so I have not moved very far. I have been blessed to work in our family business my entire life. There is nothing better than working with family and farmers. No kidding!

I have three wonderful daughters, two good sons-in-law, two good grandchildren, and a wife of twenty-eight-plus years, who deserves a medal for putting up with me. I'm the last person anybody would ever thought would have written a book. I have never gone to the library or read books, and I don't think that I have finished three books in my life. In school I just read the start of chapters and closing comments and would BS my way to a grade of C. Hopefully it will all work out.

In conclusion, hopefully my different and unique sense of humor, which my wife and daughter think is warped, will come through. I truly believe humor can be found in almost every situation. It is easy to find problems in everything, but look hard and find the humor, and you will be much happier.

Read and enjoy!

My Family
Thanksgiving 2009
Bottom, my 2 grandkids.
Middle, 3 daughters and my wife.
Back, me surrounded by my sons-in-law.

Acknowledgments

To all the farmers I have worked with over the years. They really are great people, and I know they can take the fun I am poking at them.

To all the great company and dealer personnel at meetings, the bars, and the dinners afterward, where I got a lot of my stories and great information (gossip).

To my dear friend Don, whom my customers know because he has ridden around with me on sales calls for the last fifteen years or so. I have learned many things from him (good and bad) that are in this book.

To my mother, who has always been there for me.

Also to my daughter, Jennifer, for her drawings in the book.

Finally, I really owe it all to the person who taught me life, to be honest and straightforward, how to be a great salesman, father, and everything else. I worked with him every day. Softball, bowling, dartball, fishing, golf, church, and almost everything else, I did with my father up till his plane wreck in 1988. I know Dad would have laughed his rear end (ass) off at this book!

In memory of R. L. *Schmidt*
(1932-1988)
Hope I *can make him proud.*

Dad and Mom

Chapter 1

Travels

On the road again and again and again

Company Trips (and Personal Trips)

Company Meetings

Eating Places
(very many over the years; just look at me)

Notes from the author:

This chapter is factually true to the best of my recollection and notes.

AGCO Corporation, when it is mentioned, is the Allis Gleaner Company, formed in 1988, and has grown to become one of the largest farm companies in the world based out of Duluth, Georgia (Atlanta area).

Schmidt Machine Company in Lovell, Ohio is the business started in 1926 by my grandfather; we sell a variety of items for AGCO. I sometimes refer to it as the shop or the business or the company.

The Beginning

I have been writing, listening, and living this book my whole life. I started thirty or so years ago when I started writing down the funny stories, jokes, and humorous stuff I have heard from all the parties, campouts, meetings, and sales calls I've had with farmers and decided it was time to put them in book form.

My earliest stories and jokes came from around the campfire when I was about sixteen. We used to camp in the neighbor's woods. People soon found out that after a few beers, I told lots of stories, jokes, and whatever (Mom, no beer until I was twenty-one).

It continued at company meetings. Speakers always felt that they had to tell a joke before they delivered their speech, and the jokes were usually not too good, but I could redo them and make them funny. The dinners and lunches at the meetings while traveling for the company were always a good source for stories, but the real good stuff was always at the bar afterward. The problem there is that a lot of those stories are hard to keep PG rated. Maybe I will take the jokes I can't clean up and have an R-rated sequel. (Good idea. I will make a note.)

I just started writing this book going through my mess of notes. (Ask Tom and the others at AGCO Corporation. I am a legend for my note taking.) I didn't know I had enough for a book, but every time I saw one note, it would remind me of two more things. This book just kept growing and growing, and every day I live, more things keep popping up. So I will probably be ready to start on a second book (I hope).

There is one thing I have to say after traveling through all these little towns: for the love of Pete, move your founding fathers' statues to the parks. I hate when the town square has great, big statues in the middle of it; it's a traffic nightmare! Couple of such towns I can think of that are in my area are Urbana and Mount Gilead, Ohio. I know there are more, but I can't think of them right now!

Eating Your Words Award

One of my earliest meetings I remembered was a Gehl (Gehl is a farm manufacturer of hay and forage) business meeting in the late seventies or early eighties. We were eating lunch (it seems like at meetings, it was always lunch or the bar afterward or on the airplane where all the good stories happened) when I heard this dealer tell this true story.

He said he was going to breakfast in a small town with the local sheriff. They got done eating, and the sheriff said, "You should pay for my breakfast."

The dealer asked, "Why?"

"Because you forgot about the guy coming last night to pick up the mower conditioner."

The dealer said, "I didn't have anybody coming."

Here the sheriff, in full uniform, helped a guy hook up a piece of equipment; and the guy stole it. (I bet that sheriff felt about two feet tall.) And I always wonder if the sheriff bought his breakfast!

Outdoor Fun?

Down in Florida, we were having tractor demos for the AGCO Corporation; we were out in the sticks (nowhere), so they had Porta-Johns set up for us to use. One of the dealers came back and said he almost got stuck in the Porta-John; the door almost wouldn't open. I didn't think much about it. Another dealer was standing there and heard the same story. The real funny part happened later, when the other dealer that was standing there headed over to the Porta-John. He got to it and pulled the handle, and it wouldn't open up. So he mustered up all his strength and yanked as hard as he could. The Porta-John came open, and he pulled the old lady that was trying to hold the door shut right out onto the ground spread-eagle in front of everybody. We teased the dealer for years and years at meetings, saying things like, "Good thing there's no Porta-Johns here. You are OK." (*He got the Golden Porta-John Award.*)

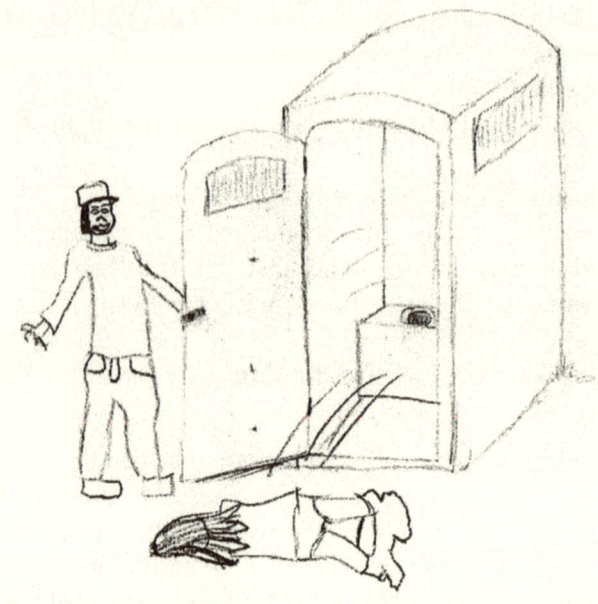

The Best Use for Duct Tape Award

A co-worker and I were heading to a new-equipment showing in Dallas, flying out of Columbus, Ohio. We got to the airport and were standing at the window, watching some people get the planes ready. They pulled up to the plane right in front of us with a ladder truck, and I thought they were going to clean the window, but they pulled a roll of duct tape out and taped it around the pilot's window.

I looked at my co-worker and said, "I am glad it is not our plane." (Our plane was the next one over.)

He said, "Why?"

I said, "Because they just put duct tape on the window!"

Just then, the pilot or co-pilot came by and said in a very serious, stern voice, "This is not duct tape, it is special aviation tape!"

I am telling you as an old farm boy who uses plenty of duct tape, just ask my wife, I was only thirty feet away, and it was duct tape!

If you are wondering, the difference between duct tape and special aviation tape is probably about fifty bucks a roll.

* * *

In another funny plane episode that happened a few years earlier, the same co-worker, my wife, other friends, and I were heading to a meeting in Vegas. We had a stopover in Minnesota, and they had to de-ice the plane. Some passengers noticed sparks coming out of the engine. The flight stewards said it was probably just ice chips from the de-icing process, but they said they would get a different plane to make us (the passengers) feel better. We went to the other end of the airport (a hard thirty-minute walk), and we boarded what we thought was another plane. Then the co-worker with me opened up the pouch in front of him, and the same gum wrapper was in the pouch that he left in the pouch on the other plane. Here they put us back on the same plane as before.

I guess they thought moving us would make us feel better, and I guess it worked; the ones in front of us complaining about the sparks seemed OK. (By the way, it was OK because we got a one-hundred-dollar voucher for another flight too!)

* * *

In yet another de-icing story, a few years earlier, this time at the Atlantic City Airport, a friend and I were sitting and listening to two very concerned women behind us; and it sounded like it was their first time flying. We were in a very heavy snowstorm, and they were de-icing the plane. In a voice loud enough for the women to hear, we started discussing what was going on. I stated that I had seen on *60 Minutes* the other night that de-icing doesn't work and that we could be in trouble. Those poor women were scared to death, and I thought they were going to get off the plane! *I know it was awfully cruel but very funny!*

Doofus Award Winner

In 1988, my wife and I and two other couples from Ohio were at a dealer meeting in the Bahamas. We had the afternoon to do what we pleased, so we rented mopeds to tool around the island. We were riding along, and one of the mopeds got a flat tire. Fortunately or unfortunately, we were right next to an old sign that said Tire Repair. So we took the moped there, and a couple of the locals said they would take care of it. One of our guys had a video camera and captured them on tape using a car jack to lift up the moped. I am glad it was not my moped because it fell one way then the other *several times* over and over. Finally, they realized the car jack wouldn't work as we were laughing our rear ends off. They finally fixed it for two dollars, and we rode a couple miles down the road, and the tire went flat again. Go figure. *(Two dollars seemed cheap till it didn't work.)*

I'm going to call Charlie and see if he still has the tape; we would probably win on Funniest Home Videos.

(Update: he has the tape and is supposed to get me a DVD copy of it!)

Lost or Found?

A co-worker and I went to a Kinze (which is a corn planter company in Iowa along I-80) meeting in Iowa sometime in the late nineties; we got in the night before the meeting like we always did. In the morning, we got up in the hotel to go to the meeting and could not find the truck keys. We searched all over the motel, searched the ground all the way to the vehicle, looked in the vehicle (from the outside since we couldn't open the door), and moved everything in the hotel room around for an hour or so. I finally said, "We are not going to get to the meeting if we don't do something." I called our Chevy dealer back home as we had a brand-new Chevy truck from there. Just as Steve answered the phone and I started to ask him how we could get a key for the truck, my co-worker moved a hat on a stand, and there was the key. I didn't know what to say, and I tried to explain what happened—badly, I might add. *I figured to this day he must have thought we really tied one on.*

Drinking and Driving and Writing Don't Mix!

One time, back in the early eighties, when a lot of people were using traveler's checks, I decided to give them a try. My wife and I were going to Vegas, and we picked up traveler's checks at our AAA (because they were free of charge, and a farm boy like me loves nothing better than free), and we were off. If you have ever been to Vegas, you know that while you are gambling, your drinks are free; and there is no drink a country boy likes better than a free one! We were in the casino most of the day (with free drinks) when I decided to cash a traveler's check with my helpful (or smart-ass) wife standing beside me, laughing her rear end off because they made me show three forms of ID because my writing didn't match what I signed earlier (before the free drinks). *Needless to say, I never took traveler's checks to Vegas again.*

Free Isn't Always Good

On the same trip, or maybe a later one, my wife and I were in Bally's Casino till what we thought was one or two in the morning; but we walked out the front, and to our surprise, it was daylight (funny how free drinks make you lose track of time). Just as we got out front, a guy rear-ended a car and shoved one car into another and then another. (He must have been in on the free drinks too.) I don't think anybody was hurt, thank goodness. The cops showed up and gave the guy a Breathalyzer test. The funny part happened when the police officer looked at the Breathalyzer. His eyes got as big as silver dollars, and he immediately handcuffed the guy. (I always wondered how high he must have blown.)

* * *

In January 2010, my wife and I got back from another successful business trip to Vegas. It was a convention with the Versatile Corporation (maker of tractors in Canada). I thought it was going to be held in Canada (imagine my disappointment), but it was held in Vegas at the Venetian, which boasts of being the largest resort in the world with seven thousand rooms!

The interesting thing was the convention going on next to ours, which was the Adult Entertainment Expo. I had to get a massage from turning my head around to look at the women going to that. (Also, my ribs were sore from my wife jabbing me!) Too bad this wasn't a convention where I left her home. (Just kidding, dear. Maybe.) They asked us if they should have the convention at the same time and location; we all said yes (at least the guys did). I am sure it had nothing to do with what was going on next door!

I also found another favorite place to eat in Vegas. (Surprise! It's a buffet!) The flavors at Harrah's—it had salad, steak, and chicken for my wife. It had a lot of seafood for me; it was all good! We were there for *Legends in Concert* (another must-see); it had Jerry Lee Lewis, Tina Turner, Bette Midler, Michael Jackson, and of course, Elvis. All looked and sounded like the original. With all these plugs, maybe they will comp me something (anything); nothing a country boy likes better than freebies!

Anyway, getting back to being informative, the biggest indication, I noticed, of the economic woes we are in was the shortage of material for the outfits those poor girls were wearing to their convention. (Darn it.)

* * *

In my younger days (not anymore, honey), on some of the business trips, we would end up in strip clubs. I started rethinking going to these places when on the west side of Indianapolis, a *very* young stripper (it seemed wrong there too because all of them looked very young) said, "How ya doin', Daddio?" I started thinking I was too old for this.

In Kansas City on an AGCO trip, we decided to go again to the strip club. So we went down to the bellhop's desk and asked them if they knew of any good places. One bellhop was fifty-five and the other seventeen maybe. The younger one spoke right up and pulled out coupons for Ziegfelds, acting like he had been there; we got a laugh out of that.

I forgot the girls that were there (other than the fact that all twelve that danced were at least a 9 1/2 or better!) but not their saying, "Ziegfelds. Nothing on but the jukebox." I took a bucket (that's what they served their beer in) from there, and it has been in my closet for the past fifteen to twenty years with that saying on it. (I'm busted; now my wife will know what it is.)

What really got me to stop going to these places started at Big Al's in Peoria, Illinois. Funny sidebar: the dealer from Fremont, Ohio that filmed the tire-change episode in the Bahamas was with me. Big Al's had three stages with girls on each one. My buddy nudged me to look across the room at the girls on the far stage, and that made the one in front of us jealous, I guess. Seemed like the place got real quiet just as she yelled, "Hey, look up here, the action is right in front of you," and everybody in the place stared at us.

I remember wondering why people were going upstairs at this place. I got home from there and told my wife exactly what went on, which I always did. She said to me, "I seen Big Al's last week on *Merv Griffin*." (That's how long ago it was). "Why was you there?" she asked me.

I said, "Just a place we all went. Why?"

Then she said, "Couples go in there to strip upstairs."

And I exclaimed, "Thank goodness I didn't go upstairs."

The real kicker was about two weeks later at a Gehl (Gehl is a farm manufacturer of hay and forage) meeting in Toledo, Ohio, we went to another strip club. I got home and told my wife as usual where I was as we were getting in bed and turned on the eleven o'clock news, and they showed that club being raided by the police. My wife looked at me, and I said, "I think it's time I quit going to these places."

Thank goodness I did quit going to these kinds of places. Because a company guy who took me to one in Indianapolis in the eighties (Brads Brass something; can't remember) moved up and is now one of the top guys in our company (AGCO). I was at the world headquarters in Atlanta, Georgia, for a meeting in the late nineties. He told me about a strip club to go to while I was down there. I didn't go; thank goodness, because that night again as I watched the news from my hotel room, they raided that place and took everybody out in handcuffs. (I've always teased him that he tried to get me arrested.)

I was on AGCO's dealer panel for taking problems from the dealer to the higher-ups (higher-ups like the president and chairman). I think my proudest accomplishment on the panel was to get them to hold more of their business meetings in Las Vegas. It worked too; the meetings there got a lot better attendance.

I want to put in a plug for another place (Maybe their business bureau will pay me. *Ha-ha*!), which is Nashville, Tennessee. Early in the twenty-first century the company had business meetings there, and I really enjoyed it. We stayed downtown next to the Rhyme Center (I believe it is the original Grand Ole Opry House). You could walk to probably twenty little honky-tonks. They would only have room for fifteen to twenty people tops. It was a whole different atmosphere than I expected. The place and people looked like they were out of the fifties and sixties, and they played what they called rockabilly. The Wild Horse Saloon was also a very interesting place too. We saw Cletus T. Judd record a show from there. I would recommend downtown Nashville to anybody. The Coyote Ugly bar was a whole other experience that I won't go into!

Took My Wife This Time

In December 2009, we went with our friends to Nashville; it was their twenty-fifth wedding anniversary. We went to the Grand Ole Opry (my first time there). In the winter, they moved to its original place downtown (great move to bring it back down there). The MC was Little Jimmy Dickens, who was about to turn eighty-nine! The show had a great mixture of old and new. Bill Anderson was there along with Trace Adkins, and Vince Gill was a surprise guest. It was my first trip, but not my last; it was very good!

The highlight of my trip, though, was our free tour of the Jack Daniel's distillery in Lynchburg, Tennessee. The downtown was well kept and looked like it did when the distillery opened in 1866! It's a dry county (believe it or not), but you could buy a commemorative bottle of Jack at the end of the tour; what more could you want (besides a beer chaser)? *Another must-see* (and it was free)!

* * *

Our Ohio, now Ohio-Michigan, dealer convention in Columbus has always been interesting. Years ago, the company and suppliers used to wine and dine with us into the wee hours, and I picked up a lot of good stories there. These days, PC (political correctness) has taken over, and not much late-hour action goes on. Dad did tell me a good story about one of the earlier conventions. He got on the elevator, and a guy (who will remain nameless) was riding up and down it with a lamp shade on his head. Dad asked him if he was drunk, and the reply was, "No, I just had too much to drink."

(I've always wondered about the difference between "drunk" and "too much to drink." *If anybody knows, send me an e-mail so I can put my mind to rest.*)

* * *

I just got back from the 2009 Ohio-Michigan Dealer Convention. I've got a question that I have wondered about for twenty-five years answered. Somebody had driven over our loading dock and landed about thirty feet out. I always wondered who was driving and what happened to the vehicle. I found out it was another dealer checking out our lot, and his truck frame broke in half. (Successful convention question answered.) That was the same guy that pulled the lady out of the Porta-John. Wait till I see him. Carlton!

Close Call

One of my first trips to Canada was with our truck driver at the shop probably in the late seventies. Massey Ferguson was closing their test facility in Toronto, and we bought a test combine and other items. I was following our semi that had the combine on it in an old two-ton truck loaded down. We were on a six-lane highway, and the combine's unloading auger came all the way out. I floored the truck but couldn't catch up, and there was a bridge coming up. I flashed my lights and finally got the truck driver to stop right before he would have hit the bridge! (Remember that, Don?)

Sometimes Half Is Better Than Whole

One meeting, somebody somewhere—don't remember where, when, or why but I remember the guy at the bar afterward—was trying to explain why he was bisexual. He said, "Think about it, you guys cut out half the population. I got the whole population to go for." (I will take my chances with half, thank you!)

Spilling the Beans

Talking about meetings, you probably know somebody in your office or have a friend who loves to let secrets out. Well, I got to know a guy that was pretty high up in AGCO at the bars after meetings; a few beers and I could always get the whole scoop on what was going on (Adrian).

Travels and Weather

I have had some very strange weather on my trips. In the early eighties, we went to Phoenix three times to introduce new equipment. It rained and rained so much (in the desert) that we couldn't go to the field demos, so they took us to the dog races. (Doggone it.)

The second trip, they had to have heaters in the tents at breakfast or we would have frozen; it was in the upper thirties every morning. (Of course they said, "It never gets this cold.") By the way, we were supposedly in the hot desert. In the evenings, (I know you will feel sorry) I would almost freeze going to the hot tub.

The third trip, we did get out to the field (unfortunately). As I was standing out there, I noticed a mountain in the distance disappear. I found out why in a couple of minutes; a terrible dust storm sent us all back to our vehicles and on our way to the hotel.

* * *

One of my first *business* trips to Las Vegas, we had snow on the strip. I asked one of the guys there if this was unusual. He said no; he remembered it snowed twelve or fifteen years ago. (Lucky me.)

The next *business* trip to Las Vegas (I need to keep this straight for the IRS), I opened my mouth and said, "We can't top the snow on the last trip." In the parking garage, I wondered why they said, "Don't park here in heavy rain." Boy, did I find out why; it looked like the Colorado River was rerouted through the parking garage as we got heavy rain (in the desert). I should have kept my mouth shut again like my wife is always telling me! E-mail me with any unusual weather.

From left: Don Plotts, Dick Pfeiffer, and me in Canada, catching my favorite fish, pike

Fishing Trips

I have been on some very interesting fishing adventures. My first trip to Canada at age sixteen was to Whitefish Falls (which is on the northeast corner of Lake Michigan). The trip began with me flying up to the falls with my dad, and when we got up there, it was foggy; we were flying at about five hundred feet, looking for the runway. Finally, we see the guy waiting for us, waving a handkerchief; man, was I glad to land. We went out at night catching catfish and drinking beer. I remember my dad was very surprised when they told him I outdrank them! (It was legal in Canada then at age sixteen. I think!)

My second trip to Canada was quite a few years later; we went on a fly-in above International Falls. I will never forget my first time on a floater plane (a Beaver). It looked like we were flying right into a mountain range; nobody else seemed excited, so I didn't say anything. We got to about a hundred yards from the cliff, and the pilot made a sharp turn right and landed in a channel—smoothly, to my relief.

The funny part of this trip happened the week before. The guy that ran the place told us what had happened. A doctor that comes every year decided to bring his secretary. The fly-ins always had a Tuesday check-in to bring supplies and check on everything. Well, the doctor's wife decided to come on the mid-week fly-in because it was their anniversary and she wanted to surprise her husband. I bet somebody was surprised because when the plane left, the doctor, his secretary, and his wife were left there for the rest of the week. (I always wondered if they got divorced or had a three-way!)

* * *

How many of you have taken your wife on a fishing trip for your honeymoon? (*Pretty redneck.*) Well, that's what I did. I don't know how I talked my wife into that. I guess she was blindly in love and just wanted to be with me. We went to Drummond Island, Michigan, and we even got some fishing in. The last day (being a country boy), I had to use up all the gas in my boat because I paid for it. With my wife watching on shore (probably wondering who she married), I trolled around the bay, using up my gas and running out of gas and losing my fishing pole in the water. I was trying to fish the line out with the paddle, losing it in the water. I looked up to the shore, and my new wife was laughing hysterically. She has reminded me over and over about how much of a cheapskate (or cheap country hick) I was for trying to use up all my gas. (Women never let you forget.)

Reminds me of when my wife and I went to an Ohio State-Michigan football game in the mid-eighties. I told my wife I wasn't paying five dollars to park. I would go up and park just off High Street in Columbus and save the five dollars. When we came back after the game and my van was gone, I thought it was stolen. Finally, I saw it was a permit-parking street, and my van was towed. My wife has reminded me over two hundred times how I saved five dollars and paid eighty-five dollars plus cab fare to get to the impound lot. (Like I said, *women never forget*.)

* * *

Back to fishing in Canada. We were on a fly-in to Kaby Lake. This turned out to be legendary. The first thing that happened was we were in shallow water about ten yards from a moose, watching it eat seaweed. I was in the back by the motor, so I turned around to watch the moose, and I noticed my foot getting wet. I had knocked the plug out of the boat and almost sunk it, but I got the plug back in just in time. (By the way, the moose can really dog-paddle; they must be able to go ten miles per hour!)

The other thing that happened on this trip has been talked about ever since. All the lakes up in there (about four hundred miles north of Sault Sainte Marie, Michigan) flow into the Hudson Bay. They have a river that comes in from the south and flows out to the north. The owner told us that on the north side where it flows out, there is a waterfall and at the bottom, a small area where fish get trapped, which was very good fishing.

We set out (two cousins of mine and a nephew) one day to go up there, and it was about twenty-five miles or so; we found it and parked to head down there. It took us probably twenty-five minutes to walk around the falls, along the ledges, and over the trees to get to the pool of water. On the second cast, one of us had a nice pike on, and we thought we had a good spot. Next thing I know, I heard some noise in the bushes, and one of the guys yelled bear; and out of the bushes came a black bear.

We were trapped between the river and another waterfall, and I thought we were going to end up in the river. I had my tackle box open; the bear went up to it, started licking inside of it, throwing several of my baits with huge hooks on them out of it. All I could think of was that he was going to get one of them in his tongue, which would make him go mad and attack us. I remember saying, "That's my tackle box, and I will fight you for it." (Must have been the farm boy in me. I didn't want to lose my tackle box.)

The one guy said later, "I always heard with grizzly bears, you stay quiet and still because they like to play with their prey. And with black bears, you make a lot of noise to scare them away." This black bear, I guess, didn't know that because my buddy started yelling and screaming, holding a two-inch knife, standing about three feet from the bear; and it didn't move or flex a muscle. The bear just didn't give a darn.

I was behind him, and all I could think of was if the bear jumped on him, I was going to pick up one of the big rocks and crack it over the bear's head. (Glad that never happened. I probably would have just pissed him off.) The bear started slowly walking down the riverbank, and it got to about thirty yards, and we picked up all our equipment to get back to the boat. The bear turned around and started chasing us out of there.

The half-hour trip to get in there over trees and long cliffs took us about five minutes to get out of there, and I ended up in the rear, carrying the landing net. The bear could have gotten us if he wanted to; it must have been busy thinking, "Look at those idiots." As I was running, I could hear it right behind us, stomping on everything as we ran.

I tripped over a tree, broke the handle off my tackle box, took the time to pick it up, and kept going. I tripped over the next tree and got my fishing net caught in the tree. All I could think of when I got the net loose was if the bear was on me, I would put the net over his head. (Wouldn't that have been a catch?)

I got up and kept going, dove into the boat, and the bear was there, staring at us. We had fished there probably a half hour, and it stood there, watching us the whole time. (*I bet the bear is still telling his buddies about that group of idiots he came across.*)

* * *

My one time on a head boat (a group fishing boat with a capacity of twenty-five or so) turned out to be a real adventure. A good friend of mine and I decided to go out on one of those group boats that go fishing in Lake Erie. I know the first exciting thing was watching the guy beside us leaning over and feeding the fish (throwing up). We fished all day and didn't catch very much, and time to go in came, and that's when the adventure started.

The captain went up to start the boat around 2:30 p.m., and nothing happened. So he radioed into shore for some batteries. The whole time, we were drifting north, away from shore. (I don't know why he didn't anchor so we didn't drift so far out.) Finally, they got out there about 4:30 p.m., put the batteries in the pit, tried to jump the boat, sparks flying. I thought they were going to blow us up.

For some reason, it didn't start. Later I heard they had starter troubles. So they had to call yet another boat to tow us in, and we were yet a couple of hours away, drifting farther out. Several interesting things were happening on the boat as daylight turned to night. We were supposed to have been in hours ago. For one thing, there were newlyweds on the boat, and I could tell she didn't want to come out there to start with, and now she was really mad because they were supposed to be staying put at the honeymoon suite (I always wondered if they stayed married, but boy, was she mad).

We called our wives, told them where we were, and about then, it got really quiet as my friend's wife said, "BS, that's where you are." And everybody on the boat heard that and started laughing. We put the captain on to try and convince them that we were still on the boat and not at a strip club.

It was creepy out there in the dark with no lights on or anything else while still drifting farther away. I thought that soon we would be in Canada. As a boat came out to tow us in, it bumped into us. One older man was scared and jumped right at me, knocking me down to get to a life vest. Again I opened my mouth and said it couldn't get any worse.

I told my buddy I had to use the john; I had an upset stomach. He said, "It just got worse, the captain just said the bathroom is out of order." I don't know how I kept from going in my pants. We finally got in at 4:00 a.m., only twelve hours late. They were handing us free coupons for another trip, and I'll never forget the guy beside me handing his back, saying, "No thanks, that was too much fun!" (If you're wondering, I took my free coupon, being a country boy.) I heard several farmers were the only ones to take the free tickets from the *Titanic*!

Watch What You Say (I Never Learn)

Me and a friend were fishing on the Sandusky River in downtown Fremont along with about one hundred people within one hundred feet. I think we were the only white people there (if you get my drift), and my friend got into some weeds. The next thing I heard him yell was, "Damn jiggers, man." I looked at him and asked, "What did you say?" He turned red when he thought about what he said, so we picked up our equipment, and we left in a hurry. (E-mail me with your fishing adventures.)

When Animals Attack! (Kinda)

Wife and I finally got our Harleys, and we have been taking as many trips as possible; what a way to see the countryside. I made a trailer so we could take a tent and some supplies (beer).

We were at a park in southeast Ohio with our bikes and some friends. We found out that if we left anything out, coons come from everywhere. I couldn't believe they went after a bag of hot Cheetos and actually fought over it, licking it clean. I got out of the tent to chase them off, yelling, "Shoo! Shoo!" And the other couples opened their tents to see what all the commotion was about, and all I heard was laughter.

First of all, I was running around in my underwear, shooing coons away and, as they have told me one hundred times since, in pink underwear. I threw them away; and by the way, they were originally red, but after washing them one hundred times in our hard water, they faded to pink. I tried to explain that, but they just kept laughing anyway.

I was down to the restroom the next morning. I heard about a family that came in the night before and left chips and other food out. They woke up to fifteen to twenty coons all over their campsite, and the kids were terrified, so they packed up in the middle of the night and left. Coons are overrunning rural areas in part because PETA and other animal groups demonize people who wear fur, so they no longer have any value.

Another animal encounter my friends won't let me forget centered around a hay elevator. I was moving it at my friend's house when two possums came out of it and brushed my leg, so I chased them with a shovel. This all happened while my friend was in the house, getting us a cool drink (beer). As my wife tells me all the time, I should think before I speak. My buddy came out, so I started to explain (without thinking what I was saying) what happened. I said two possums came out of the elevator, and I chased them all around, banging them (forgot to add with a shovel) all over the place; you can imagine how he explained that story.

Well, I have been through moose, beer, coons, and possums so far. On to dogs. I'm glad nobody had seen what happened. I was at a farmer's place north of North Baltimore, Ohio. I stopped and walked up to the door; nobody was home, so I started back for the station wagon, and here came a Doberman. I knew I couldn't open the car door, so I jumped on top of the car. The next fifteen to twenty minutes (seemed like hours), I tried to get down and in the car door, but the dog wouldn't let me. Finally, he got far enough away for me to get in the car. (It crossed my mind to run it over.)

My animal problems began at six or seven with a pony we got. We should have known better because we were at a picnic at the farm of the pony's previous owner (Lew), who gave the pony to us right after it took a bite out of his truck seat. That pony wouldn't do anything; we would drag it down the road to the railroad and hop on for dear life, and it would fly back to the barn. The worst problem was it would go under a tree limb in Grandpa's yard to try and knock you off if you were still on; it would then brush up against a barbwire fence. (It was a good candidate for dog food. Or glue!)

We had horses for years and never really had any major problems. I was at our fair walking past a horse when it kicked sideways, right into my belt buckle. I hate to think what would have happened if its kick was a couple of inches lower, and I don't mean to me but to that horse; it might have been dog food real quick! We finally got out of horses, so I turned our barn into a party house; besides, drinking beer sounds one H of a lot better than shoveling manure.

My neighbor Shorty had cows he milked and is quite the storyteller. If I told him, "Boy, it's cold," instantly he would say something like, "Oh, this nothing. Forty-two years ago, it was a lot colder." So I never did know if he was telling me stories or not.

He would milk about seventeen cows; he told me each cow would come when he called their name. I didn't believe it till I saw him do it. I would point at a cow. Shorty would call its name; it would perk up its ears and come. Each cow had its own stall; he broke his arm and had to go to the hospital, and some relations that had milked cows for many years came to milk them. I probably was only nine or ten, so they weren't going to listen to me.

I told them, "Good luck, his cows only go in certain stalls." They laughed at me until they couldn't get the cows to go in the stalls, milk, eat, or do anything else; then they were swearing, screaming, and throwing stuff.

Fortunately for them or the cows, I don't know which, Shorty came home from the hospital and showed them which stall they would go in! (E-mail me with any of your animal stories.)

Snowmobile Trips

I first went up to Michigan with Dad and Mom in 1969 to Grayling in the Lower Peninsula; back then, that was as far north as people would go. We drove MF Ski Whizes, of course, because that was what we sold. I remember my sister, my cousin, and me, all three on a 500SS long-track sled; what an adventure.

I first took my wife and two daughters up in 1988, and we were on a pair of '79 Scorpion TKs. (Surprise! That was what we sold.) I figured if they liked it, we were going to have to update our sleds. We were sitting on our sleds outside a restaurant in Lovell, Michigan, which is between Gaylord and Grayling (same size as Lovell, Ohio, where I live—two businesses and a couple of houses) when a couple of guys looked over and said, "Look at those antique sleds." (Then I knew I had to update.)

Elevator to Nowhere
(Hope my wife doesn't read this.)

We were snowmobiling in Paradise, Michigan, when this next story took place; wife and I were staying at a place called Heidi's Traveler (by the way, I was just up there and had seen it close up like half of the other places in the Upper Peninsula) when we went across to the Best Western to see the rest of our group. We used to stay there in cabins till they decided it cost too much to heat them, and they closed them and built the Best Western.

Anyway, setting this story up, you enter the hotel on the second floor; the first floor is down on the beach level. I told my wife the group was on the second floor, and I went on ahead of her. I was sitting in the room when my wife, Lori, came in; and she said the strangest thing. Quote: "You got a quiet elevator here."

We all looked at her and said, "Why did you get on the elevator? You came in on the second floor." She (I hope doesn't kill me) went on to put her foot in her mouth and say, "No wonder it was so quiet. I went in on the second floor, pushed second floor, and got right back off." My wife continued to wade in deeper and deeper; she said, "I wondered why they had a check-in desk on both floors, and there was a kid standing there when I got on, and why he ran up to the second floor and was standing there when I got off." I always figured that kid's been laughing and telling that story ever since. (We sure have been.)

* * *

I'm not sure if it was the same trip or another one (the older you get, everything seems to run together), but our good friends (also the ones we bike with) were at Heidi's Traveler too. They went to leave, and the truck their boy had driven up had fuel-line freeze-up and wouldn't start; my friend was really mad because he told his boy not to let it sit empty on fuel. So picture this: they hooked up their truck to their big four-place snowmobile trailer and pulled the other truck with a rope.

I figured they wouldn't get very far; believe or not, they got almost two hundred miles downstate before a state policeman stopped them in the lower peninsula of Michigan. My buddy told the policeman, "We just started pulling it and was heading for the next exit." The patrolman said, "I got reports from a couple of counties back about you." (He didn't tell them he had come two hundred miles!)

What I can't believe is they didn't get stopped at the Mackinac Bridge (*which is the longest suspension bridge in the world—five miles* [more education]) toll booth. I said, "What did you say at the toll booth?" And my friend said, "I am paying for the truck behind me." (And I bet they didn't know it was being pulled by a rope!)

* * *

My next story happened at Paradise, Michigan, again; this time, it was around zero, and we were riding toward Lake Superior to a remote place called Rainbow Lodge. I was riding behind everybody else when I got a good idea (or it seemed like it to me); to the surprise of our group, I had stopped, took my jacket and shirt off, and rode bare-chested (remember it is zero). The funniest thing was looking at the people in the restaurant staring in disbelief! (As usual, my wife was very proud of me.)

I know cold must not bother me too much because we camped with our friends in Waters, Michigan. In the winter, so we couldn't have any water in our camper, we needed to walk up to the shower house in the mornings. One such morning, we were heading there (I was in shorts and a T-shirt) and commented, "Boy, it's cold." We got up there and looked at the thermometer; it was forty-two below zero! (*It was a dry cold, though.*) Brrr!

* * *

Couple of years ago, we were again in the Upper Peninsula of Michigan when this episode took place at a bar called Bear's Den. This was a guy's trip with my cousin and his boy; my wife's sled was newer, so I rode hers for the trip. I was sitting on my sled waiting for them when a couple of guys walked by, staring all the way past. They were looking at each other and whispering. I couldn't figure out why till I got out on the trail, remembering what my wife's sled said on the front. (*Badass girls drive badass toys.*)

* * *

On a more serious note, snowmobiling is a dangerous sport; a lot of people kill themselves every year, most of them by missing a curve and hitting a tree. People don't think. We came upon a wreck; they had just taken the guy away. He had hit a tree on a straight stretch. I asked his buddy what happened. It was his first day snowmobiling, and he had bought a 1000 sled like his buddy had (I been sledding for forty years and have a 600 that will hit 90 in 100 yards). He was probably going 120 and lost control.

My daughters and cousins had just started riding, and we were trying to get them to listen to us and stay to the far right on the trails, especially on the curves. We heard about a wreck the day before; two sleds collided at a curve, and one got killed (and it wasn't the one that was drunk). It was close to where we were going, so we went by to show the kids. It was horrible; we saw pieces of helmet and parts of the sled. The worst part was that the snow for ten feet around the wreck was red from the blood! I hope it made them think; it sure did me!

Years ago, everybody took booze out with them on the trail. I was no exception, but fortunately, most of us got wiser and quit that. Good thing because one day, a ranger stopped and asked me to say my ABC's. I couldn't figure what he said, and said, "What did you say?" The guy behind fell off his sled laughing, saying, "He told you to say your ABC's." I didn't expect that; good thing I wasn't drinking because he sure probably thought I had been!

* * *

I am going to tell you about eating places later, but I will tell you about some unusual ones I have run into while snowmobiling, like Rainbow Lodge (where I rode into with no shirt on); it has no electricity and runs on wind and generators. The one I am going to tell you about next, most of you will not be able get to; it's thirty miles from nowhere, south of Grand Maris in the UP of Michigan on the trail. The guy is out there all winter, selling hotdogs, soups, and such; we always make it a point to stop out there.

In 2008, we, as usual, stopped out there for coffee; and along came a group of kids with the girls wearing dresses. That was the first time I had seen that in all my years of snowmobiling. When they left, we asked the guy there who that was. He said, "They come out there all the time from the local Mennonite Church. (Remember, it's thirty miles from anywhere.) *Brrr!*

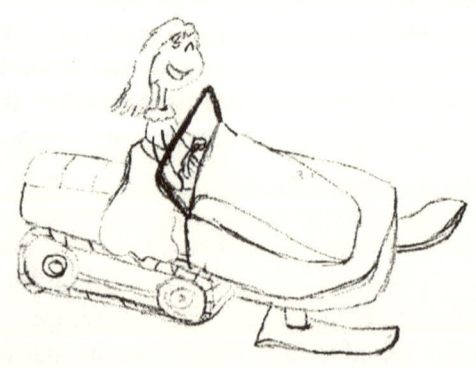

We were getting ready to go on a snowmobile trip the next day, and we took a little ride on our sleds. We started across our local pond, and it was a little slushy on top. My wife panicked, thought she was falling through, and floored it all the way to the bank, hitting the side too hard, bending the ski back, and flying off. I got there (sticking my foot in my mouth again) saying, "What did you do to the sled? We leave tomorrow."

She got mad, saying, "You're more worried about the sled than me."

I said, "I could see you were OK," but my wife still tells everybody I was more worried about the sled than her. (I probably deserve it too.)

* * *

My newest son-in-law had never been on a snowmobile (probably never will again); we talked my daughter and him into going with us last winter (January 2009). We went to Gaylord in the lower peninsula of Michigan and rode out toward Starvation Lake. I opened my mouth (again), saying how good the old snowmobile (1997 Ski-doo 2 up) was running; it had just climbed the hills at an old ski resort. We were just putting fuel in it at Starvation Lake when my son-in-law, while going down the trail, saw fire coming out of the dash. He pulled over, and it burned up completely, with a whole circus of people coming by taking pictures.

The funniest part was that when I pulled up, my wife and son-in-law were nowhere to be seen; here they had gone a half a mile down the trail because, as my wife stated, "On TV, things blow up real big!" I told him not to worry; I would only hold this over his head for twenty or thirty years.

(This is the picture we put up at work on the bulletin board since he works at Schmidt's with me, or at least he did!)

picture of sled burning up

This is how far they drove away!

E-mail me with any good snowmobile stories

Eating Places

Anybody that knows me knows I love to eat, especially buffets. I have been blessed by meetings, company trips, vacations, and whatever to eat at many unique places, starting right at our shop; we have the Lovell Market to eat at. Friday, for as long as I can remember, has been Fried Bologna Day. We had an AGCO rep who couldn't believe how wound up we got about bologna. One reason was because he lived by Waldo, Ohio. Their claim to fame is G-R Bar and its bologna sandwich also (I would highly recommend it too, by the way). Over the years, he has moved up in the company and now is one of the top guys. I call him every once in a while on Fridays to tell him it's Bologna Day across the road. I have thought about UPS-ing Tom a bologna sandwich just for the fun of it.

I should start with my food from my school days. I was up to almost ten names for the same sandwich (none with four letters): Chuckwagon, Salisbury steak, hoagie, chopped steak, and hamburger are some of the names; I can't remember all the names I had for the *same sandwich*. One very different one was a soy burger, and it was awful!

Farmers and dealers can be real rednecks. I was in southeastern Ohio (which is basically like West Virginia) at a cookout and field demo to drive new tractors. I saw something I had never seen before: the dealer's brother stomped a ground hog to death. If you don't know, ground hogs follow the same path back to their hole. He got in the path and cut off the ground hog and literary kicked it to death. (After that, I wondered what the meat was at the cookout!)

Huddle in Crestline on old US 30 (Lincoln Highway) was a great place for a steak. It looked kind of run-down from the outside. I had sent Mom there, telling her about the steaks. She had seen the place from the outside, almost didn't go in, but they did and had a great meal. Besides steaks, they had good stuffed shrimp, the likes I haven't had since they closed; and every time I was in there, they had the same old lady playing the piano.

A place most of you couldn't find with GPS is Bullwinkle's in Dola, Ohio. Also a tough-looking place on the outside (inside too), but very good all-you-can-eat fish-and-salad bar. (So I was told. Ha-ha!)

Place I ate at twice, in the early '80s and again in 2005, north of Scottsdale, Arizona, is called Pinnacle Peak. A great view from high up. The best part is that AGCO is going to keep going there for classroom and field time in their tractors, so I am sure I will be there again. One of their claims to fame is two million or so neckties on the ceiling: if somebody wears a tie in, they cut it off. One of the early times I was there, apparently not everybody knew that because I saw a well-dressed gentleman get very mad when his tie was cut off. If you are in the area it would be a good place to go. (Can't tell you about the price since AGCO paid for it. Darn it.)

I am writing this story down on Thanksgiving Day 2008 as I am getting ready for another family dinner. The ones on my side are subdued compared to the one on my in-laws' side. We get into some very lively discussions on politics, schools, and most everything else. Politics especially since I am far right and they're far left; even though they're politically messed up, they're still good people.

Another unusual smorgasbord was at Miramar Air Force Base in San Diego, California, in a hangar. (Very nice since AGCO picked up the tab too! Free is always good!) In MGM Studios in Florida, after it closed, we had a smorgasbord set up right on the midway; and they kept several rides open for us, including the Tower of Terror. My youngest daughter kept wanting to ride it; the worst problem was we had just eaten. About the fourth time of the elevator dropping straight down, I thought my stomach was coming straight up! The hotel they kept us in was right on Disney ground; it was the one where they show their tram running through. It was very nice.

(And the best part was AGCO was paying for it. Double darn it.)

Another unusual smorgasbord was set up at the Horse Whisperer Ranch close to Michael Jackson's Neverland Ranch. We had a very intense demonstration on breaking a wild horse while we ate. The guy who gave the demonstration has been on TV specials and wrote books on his thirty-minute technique of breaking a wild horse, and it was very interesting, to say the least! (The best part was that it was free again, care of AGCO. Are you detecting a pattern here?)

Of all 1,228 smorgasbords (give or take one or two), the biggest one was at the riverboat in Kansas City. It had five or six stations of different countries' food (about the fourth country, I was ready to explode). Another great place to go. (Best part? AGCO paid. Although I liked this one so well I went back and paid myself, but not on the same day!)

I am writing this during the Pittsburgh-Baltimore championship game on January 18, 2009. As Martina McBride sings the national anthem, it made me remember something. Not only did the KC trip show me the best strip joint, the biggest smorgasbord, but it also had the best entertainment of any business trip, Martina McBride. (AGCO is cheap, so I know it was before she hit it big.) I shook her hand, and her career really took off. (My wife says I'm nuts.)

We even plan our trips so we can stop at buffets, and casinos usually have good ones. (By the way, I like all buffets; some are just better than others!)

For example, on our annual trip to the Kinze meeting (which, by the way, has the best lunch of any business trip—a steak dinner by the Iowa Cattlemen's Association, which the company's daughter stopped when she took over) we stayed at the Isle of Capri Casino on the way home. Guess why. Believe it or not, a good buffet and a little beer and gambling!

Back to the Kinze meeting in Williamsburg, Iowa, a little town of five hundred or so. We had to look hard, but we found what we wanted—a buffet, or at least kind of. On Thursday night (luckily, that's the night we got in town), the local (*only*) bar-and-pizza place had one-dollar drafts and free pizza. I thought I was in heaven! We went there several years in a row, but I am not sure if it is still there or not. But knowing us, we will find something else if it is gone!

My personal favorite smorgasbord (not my wife's at all) is Schmidt's in German Village in Columbus, Ohio. (No relation, by the way. Darn it.) They have been there so long (one hundred years or so); the restaurant is in the middle of the street. My friends are amazed how I tell them I don't know where it is, but I always drive right to it, despite all the streets being very narrow and looking the same.

Schmidt's Bahama Mama sausage is as close to the perfect food as it gets. (In fact, I think it is what the disciples had at the last supper and the pilgrims had at the first Thanksgiving.) Schmidt's is a good German spread of kraut, cabbage, fried onions, stewed sausage, garlic knockers, three (yes, three) kinds of Bahama Mamas (hot, hotter, hottest), and lots more! (It's a must-go-to.)

Even my business meetings revolved around smorgasbords! We had our MF dealer meetings with the surrounding dealers on Monday nights at the poor house in my local town, which is Upper Sandusky, Ohio, till one dealer found out they had all-you-can-eat walleye on Wednesdays, so we had to move our meetings to—guess what—Wednesdays. That dealer was one of the biggest eaters (besides my son-in-law; yes, you) that I ever met and is the same one that pulled the lady off the john by the way!

We would be on a dealer trip, have a big banquet at six o'clock or so; by ten he was ready for pizza and beer. (No kidding.) Just an interruption: as I am writing this, my wife came by with a new ornament for the Christmas tree (given to me by one of my smart-ass friends)—a bear with a fishing pole; they will never let me forget the bear chasing.

Back to smorgasbords. Last year I stopped at Wilmington, Ohio, on the south side along US 68.

I forgot the name of it, but it was very good. They told me it was the original Duffs (a chain in these parts for years), but it was not called that now.

Vegas is just one gigantic smorgasbord, but they're sure not $2.99 like when my wife and I first started going out there. My favorite buffet is at the Rio; it's expensive, thirty dollars the last time I was there, but where else can you eat all the crab and shrimp nine different ways and all the lobster you want?

I figured with the price of lobster at home, I ate probably one hundred dollars' worth! Off the subject—again, and the guys will like this—Rio gets my vote for best barmaids' outfits (three ounces)!

Fitzgerald downtown (Vegas) is a small buffet but very good. Again off the subject, but it's my favorite place to play roulette. Just ask my wife. I got hot playing there. (Didn't help or hurt, depending on whose view, but a gal from California kept rubbing over me to play her chips. Darn it.) We started playing about 8:00 p.m. We thought it was about midnight; here it was 4:00 a.m. when we finished! (What more can I say than, "Free drinks"?)

It's not a buffet (darn it) but the portions are big at the Harley Cafe on the strip; very unique, a must-go, even if you're not a Harley person.

Around our area, Hong Kong buffets are my favorite. They not only have good Chinese but a lot of seafood, and every time I go, I say it's my last because I stuff myself silly.

In one of my prouder all-you-can-eat displays was with my father and brother-in-law; we took credit for making our local LK Restaurant stop their all-you-can-eat perch on Friday nights. One night, the three of us had sixty-four pieces of perch; they canceled it before the next week!

(E-mail me with your favorite buffet story.)

The snowmobile trips have turned up many good places to eat in Michigan. Like the stand in the middle of nowhere south of Grand Maris I told you about earlier. Speaking of Grand Maris, it has two good eating places in it; one brews its own beer. There are a lot of microbreweries in Michigan. (By the way, there are no bad microbrews, just some better than others.)

Tahquamenon Falls by Paradise is a great restaurant brewery. If you get there, walk down to the falls; it is well worth it. Plus you will get your exercise. The sign is correct; there are ninety-nine steps. (I counted them!)

Big Buck Brewery in Gaylord at Exit 182 off I-75 has good food and microbrewed beers too!

Lovell's, which I told you about earlier, has a good restaurant and a bar restaurant in it (the only two businesses in town). Larry's 7 Ski Inn west of Gaylord by the Jordan River Valley has been very popular with snowmobiles. I'll never forget my first trip heading to Larry's, when I hit my first lake-effect snow heading across the wide-open potato fields before I got to Larry's.

If you have never seen lake-effect snow up there, it's unbelievable; the sun can be shining one moment and snowing so hard the next you can't see. Well, I had never seen it before, and it started. I had to stop because I couldn't see ten feet away! It was scary. I didn't know if it would last two minutes, two hours, or two days. It stopped about fifteen minutes and ten inches of snow later, and was I glad to get to Larry's.

Newberry in the Upper Peninsula has a good place called Timber Charlie's; the ribs there are worth stopping for. Off the subject yet again, but on our last trip, we stopped at Timber Charlie's (by the way, I had a great bowl of potato soup). It was three o'clock in the afternoon. There were just two separate groups in there, and I knew both of them; they were from Ohio and were farmers. My wife and I decided if we were going to cheat on each other we'd have no idea where to go since we were always finding somebody we knew! We have probably eaten at one hundred or so bars in Michigan, and most had good food. (You can tell I like most foods; some are just better than others!)

A very unique place in the Upper Peninsula of Michigan is a bar in Hulbert; while you eat, deer are eating just a few feet away. You're watching them through glass as they eat, run around, and do what they do! (Kids or anybody, it's a must-see.)

Frederic Inn just north of Grayling, Michigan, has very good Mexican food; and I can vouch for it because I have tried everything in there. Swamp 2 across the road from the inn is the place most snowmobilers go. I did some asking why it was called Swamp 2; the first Swamp was destroyed by a tornado in the '70s. Back in the Upper Peninsula, the most popular food is called a pasty. Basically, it's dough wrapped around pot roast, vegetables, and other things; very good. (Not what I thought of when I heard "pasty" either.)

For fish, they all want to serve you whitefish caught in Lake Superior. I love all fish, just some better than others, but that fish has a very strong taste. It's got a dark streak running through it like a sheep's head does around home. Stay with walleye, perch, cod, and you will be much happier.

Munising, also in Lake Superior, has several good places to eat; one of them, the Dog Patch, was voted number one snowmobile restaurant in the United States. (It's good. I don't know if I would vote it number one). On Friday, it has—guess what—a seafood buffet! (Did I ever tell you I like all buffets but just some better than others?)

Red Flannel Inn in Paradise is a good place to eat; it's in front of the Best Western. Jim and his crew do a good job. Jim knows us there as the Scorpion Gang because back then in our group, all rode Scorpion snowmobiles, and we had about eight of them! (We rode them—guess why—because that was what we sold.)

Restaurant, Lounge & Gift Shop
325 E Superior St, Munising, MI 49862

ɔyenterprises.com • (888) 229-6084

Just north of Paradise is Whitefish Point. Just offshore is where the *Edmund Fitzgerald* went down. It's really neat at the point; ice piles up from the wind blowing in (Superior never freezes because it is the deepest of the Great Lakes, I think 1,200 feet at some point; that's darn deep). It's no eating place, so I don't know why I mention it now.

Starvation Lake Bar west of Grayling is a nice stop to eat at (not to mention the only stop). They have a funny picture of a guy snowmobiling naked on the wall. (I hope alcohol was involved.) I know all the food stops on the way north along I-75 and US 23; one must-stop going north is Tony's at Exit 136 along I-75, you'll never go hungry. My wife and I decided to share the omelet, which was a good idea. We had our fill and took the rest home for two more meals' worth. We asked the waitress how many eggs were in it. She said normally eight, but ours looked like it had twelve, and believe it or not, their prices were normal! (I would like to see the *Man v. Food* guy take on this place!)

The Marathon at Exit 17 off of US 23 next to Cabals has hundreds of kinds of beef jerky; my favorite, which I'm eating right now, is venison and hot pepper cheese. (A real country hick can fill up on the twenty or so samples they always have out!)

Prices of food, fuel, lodging, and most everything else is higher in the Upper Peninsula; but I am sure it costs more to get stuff out there (in the sticks). But it is worth going to the Upper Peninsula of Michigan if you get a chance. Eating in Michigan or around home, if I have time, I would rather eat at a local place than a chain (even though people at the shop, and customers too, think I know every McDonald's around; that's why my cell phone says, "Leave message. I am at McDonald's").

Tony Paco's Restaurant in Toledo, Ohio (made famous on the TV show *M*A*S*H* by Clinger), is a must-see. It has thousands of hot dog buns on the wall signed by presidents and all kinds of other celebrities. Their Hungarian hot dogs are also very good. (So I was told! Ha-ha!)

My only trip to New York City, we ate at Spiro's Pizza at Times Square, but parking when we got there was what was more interesting. We got out of my van; all nine of us started walking when we saw a couple of guys standing by a car. One guy had a long chain for a necklace. All of a sudden, a guy pops his head up from inside a car and yells, "I got it!" They drove off with the car siren going off. I looked at my wife, ready to go get in the van and get out of there, but we stayed to eat at Times Square. The whole time I was eating, though, I was wondering if my van would be there when we got back.

Summing it up, all in all I like to eat! My wife says, "No kidding." (I like all food, just some better than others.)

Enjoy Chapter 2!

Chapter 2

True Stories

About Farmers, Me, and Others

Words of Wisdom, Quotes, and Sayings
(I heard mostly from farmers)

My grandson and me after he dared me to cut my hair like his.

Notes from the author:

This chapter is factually true to the best of my recollection and notes I took over the years.

Practical Thinking Training

My grandson, now eight, was riding around with me on sales calls; and I thought I would try to make him think. We went by a cemetery, so I asked him how many were dead in there. He said, "I don't know." I told him, "All of them!"

We went by an even bigger cemetery, so I asked my grandson again, "How many are dead in there?" He said, "It's too big to count, Grandpa." Again I replied, "All of them."

A little later again, we went past another cemetery. I said, "Jordan, how many are dead in there?" He thought a little, laughed, and said, "All of them, Grandpa." I thought to myself, *Now he is thinking*. (My daughter thinks my training is strange; what do you think?)

Before I get started on the other stories, I just want to say that after raising three daughters, raising a grandson is a whole different ordeal. My grandson is always trying to make up jokes because he says he wants to do comedy with me (bless his heart). His favorite joke is, why does Santa have such a good garden? Because he *ho-ho-hos*!

There Is A Difference!

My grandson Jordan was on a sales call on a remote back road, and he said, "I got to go number one, where can I go?" I stopped the car and said, "Alongside of the truck." He thought that was the greatest thing. I got to thinking the girls wouldn't go outside for any reason.

They Do Pick Up Things!

I delivered a new red tractor one day with my grandson. We got there; he told the farmer, "We brought you a nice new shiny red MF tractor, not like that ugly green one over there." I never told him, but he picked up that I wasn't a fan of John Deere. (This story is about Ron Cole, a good friend who gave me a lot of good jokes over the years; he died suddenly on January 20, 2010. I will miss your stories, bud.)

Miracle Recovery!

He was complaining about his ears hurting, and his hearing wasn't very good, so his mom took him to the doctor. After the checkup, the doctor told him and his mom he needed tubes in his ears. His response was, "Won't that hurt? My ears are fine, and I can hear OK now."

* * *

I heard he threw up at school, so I asked Jordan what happened; he said, "I don't know, but it looked like my lunch." I asked him when he threw up, and he said, "Right after lunch. I threw up ravioli, and it even had little chunks of the meatballs in it." (Thanks, Jordan, I really needed to know that!)

* * *

It was grandparents' week to eat with their grandchildren at school. Jordan asked me what day I was coming, and I asked him, "Why do you want to know?" His response was, "So I can tell them to have a beer ready for you, Grandpa!" (A little too helpful.)

* * *

Last year, we were delivering a mower about dusk, and three deer ran out in front of us; they turned around and ran right back into the woods. I said, "Jordan, we sure scared those deer." He said, "We sure did. I think they peed on the road!"

* * *

Last year his mom had to take clean pants to him at school, so I asked Jordan what happened.
"I thought I had to fart, Grandpa, but I had an upset stomach, and it ran out!"
He was with me a couple days later. I heard him fart. I said, "Jordan, you just farted."
He goes, "I know. It's great. I can fart again and not worry." (Grandchildren are great; you can spoil them and send them home!)

* * *

Farmers aren't liars, but like fishermen, they like to stretch the truth. One farmer, when I asked him what his yield was, told me, "Can't tell you. Haven't been to the coffee shop to hear my neighbors' yield yet." (Remember when you told me that, Dave?)

* * *

Another good old honest farmer always acted like he forgot the price I gave him on a piece of equipment, so I would always raise the price; boy, that would jar his memory! We had a lot of fun with that. (Right, Doyle?)

* * *

One good boy (actually, more than one) always tried to act poor to work me over on price; he would say, quote, "My ground is so poor, the crows carry knapsacks when they fly over."
(You know who you are, don't you?)

Farmers never want you to think they have money unless they don't. Then they want you to think they do! (That applies to more than farmers.)

Guys, don't lie to your wives because, believe me, it will come back to haunt you. I sold a new combine to a farmer, and he told his wife he had just waxed the old one, thinking he would tell her later. Big mistake. Guy came up to him at a Little League game, asking about his new combine; well, it hit the fan right there! (It always catches up, doesn't it, Lynn, old buddy?)
Real funny sidebar to this story happened later that night when he called me at home. I thought he was going to tell me he needed a place to stay, but he was calling for another reason. I told him, "Always tell your wife when you're buying something because I don't want to be the cause of a divorce."

Don't go against your wife's wishes either; there will be hell to pay! One company rep that called on me did, and he probably is still hearing about it today! His wife told him not to buy a sailboat, but he did anyway. Somehow he talked her into going out with him for the first and *only* time as the sailboat flipped over as soon as they started and they drifted for hours waiting for help. (I am sure his wife hasn't forgotten that.)

Wives Don't Forget!
(Just ask mine.)

Talking about wives not forgetting, my wife again brought up about trying to save five bucks on parking. I talked about it in the last chapter when I had to pay an eighty-five-dollar tow fee. (Like I said before, forget it, Lori.)

Under the Heading of Bad Photography, on Several Levels!

We were on a cruise in the Bahamas when we decided to go snorkeling, and we rented an underwater camera. I took several pictures, and so did Lori. We got home; we took them to our parents to see. Well, I took one of Lori, and all I got was her dark bathing suit. Well, when her mom looked at it, she said, "Is that a manatee?" Well, that was bad enough. Then we got to my mom's, and she said, "Is that a manatee?" My first mistake (not my last) was that I laughed and laughed; she accused me of telling my mom to say that. Needless to say, that picture is long gone. (After telling this, I might need a place to stay!)

Genius!

While I'm getting in deeper and deeper, I'll tell one I know my wife doesn't know I'm putting in this book about her. We were taking golf carts home after a long weekend camping when I told my wife, "I loaded the three-wheel cart, I will come back for the four-wheel golf cart." My wife said the strangest thing. "You only got three boards." After I laughed for ten minutes, I explained I didn't need another board! (I love you, honey.)

This part is for blondes only: if you're wondering why the four-wheeler didn't need another board, it's because the back wheels line up with the front; hence, only two boards are needed.

Wives Can Ruin the Moment
(Just ask mine again!)

We were again at *the* Ohio State at a football game; it was a big victory, so we went to Hineygate to celebrate, which is a big party out in front of the Holiday Inn on campus. Things were getting out of control, and college girls were flashing us out of windows up above. The crowd (including me) was yelling, "Take it off." My wife poked me, saying, "That could be your daughter someday." I said, "Thanks, you sure ruined that moment!" (Funny thing is now, twenty years later, my daughter is a freshman at Ohio State.)

I did learn a lesson after this happened, though; that was to *not* take my wife anymore. (Just kidding, Lori, that's not really why I haven't taken you back. *Oops*.)

* * *

I know a farmer by a little town of Wharton who let his buddy use his truck for the first and probably the last time to go to a junkyard to get some parts. On the way was an adult bookstore and massage parlor; his buddy stopped there, took a picture of his truck in front of the sign, and mailed it to his wife! (Nice buddy.)

* * *

I continue to be a big Ohio State fan, and I have been to Wisconsin games several times (mainly because their coach, Dave McClain, was from my hometown); and boy, do they party up there, win or lose! I knew some local farmers that were heading up there in a camper. They stopped at the roadside rest, and when they left, one guy was still in the john, and they didn't realize he was missing till they were fifty miles down the road. (Reminds me of the old joke: "If anybody is missing, raise your hand.")

With *friends* like these, who needs enemies?

* * *

I am writing this book not to offend people, not necessarily to be politically correct either, but hopefully, to be humorous. (The country is way too serious these days.)

Politically Correct

I was surprised that PC even hit our rural doctor's office. I was just in for my annual physical (actually, only my second since high school), and a $150 office visit later, all the doctor could say was, "You're weight challenged." At this point, I was happy for PC because up till now, I thought I was a *fat ass*! (That's a true story, and stories based on truth always get the best laugh in my stand-up comedy.)

* * *

I'm writing this as I head on to yet another business trip—this time to Heston, Kansas—in December 2008. It's starting out great, hurrying at the security point while pulling off my belt. I ripped it in two!

I can just picture myself standing in front of company personnel, mooning them (not a pretty sight, one even my wife doesn't want to see!)

Update: I did make it home without losing my pants (thank God)!

Talking about traveling, if it has happened once, it's happened one hundred times. I tell somebody I'm from Upper Sandusky, they'll say they like the rides at Cedar Point. We are south of Sandusky, about sixty miles upstream on the Sandusky River. I guess that's why we are south but called Upper Sandusky.

Back in the '70s, our school band traveled to New York to the Macy's Day Parade despite telling them several times, when our big moment came on TV, that we were from—guess were—Sandusky, Ohio.

Just the other day, I heard sports announcer Jim Jackson talking about our local star on the Ohio State basketball team, John Diebler. He said, "I like the rides at Cedar Point, John's hometown." Jim should know better; he is from Toledo, just thirty miles west of Sandusky, where Cedar Point is, and sixty miles north of us here in Upper Sandusky.

(Author's tip: investors, our town would be a good place for an amusement park since everybody thinks we got one anyway!)

Moving on, the generation that lived through the Great Depression (which could be us now) hated to get rid of anything. Farmers are no different; I am selling to the sons or grandsons of the ones that lived through it. Their barns were full of everything; their dads thought there could be a use for them and would not throw them out.

It was no different at our shop; Grandpa started the business in the '30s, never wanted to get rid of anything. I remember my dad and my uncle saying, "Wait till he goes to Florida. We'll junk it then." (I always wondered what Grandpa thought when he got home and the stuff was gone.)

Ask What You Mean

I was with Dad on a sales call when I was twelve or so when he pulled up to a stop sign and asked me how the weather was. Well, I always have been interested in weather, so I was looking up at the sky and said, "Looks

OK." Dad was of course talking about the traffic; he pulled out, missing a truck by about two inches. So ask what you mean!

April Fools

My neighbor called down back when we had horses and said one was loose; we said, "Thanks, we'll go get him." I remembered it was April 1 and figured he was trying to pull an April Fools joke, and sure enough, he was because the horse was in the barn.

I had my daughter go and get the horse; she took it down the road to his barn, which was across the road from his house. We had him on a long line so it looked like the horse was loose in the field. I called the neighbor and said, "Thanks for telling me. He was loose, but you should've told me he was across the road from your house in the field."

He got all excited, saying he was just joking and didn't know the horse was loose; that's when I said, "April Fools!" to him. He said, "I will never try an April Fools joke on you again!" *Gotcha, Dave!*

* * *

Talking about horses on the loose, we had one of the best stories ever! We put a hood on our horse's head to keep it warm, to keep away its winter hair so we could take it to shows. The hood moved, covering the horse's eyes, so it couldn't see; and it walked right through the fence. It ended up at our neighbor's house; they called us at about 4:00 a.m. My wife got off the phone and said our neighbor went into the bathroom, looked up, and the horse was looking at him. I said, "What?" thinking she was dreaming. Here our horse, wandering aimlessly, ended up with his head against their bathroom window! (How would you like that in the middle of the night?)

Thirsty Farmer or Tractor?

I live three houses down from where our family came over from Germany in the 1850s and built the house that is still there, so I haven't moved too far in my life. When we got married, my wife didn't want to live in the country, so we bought a place in town. I finally got a chance to buy my sister's house in Lovell and got my wife out of town for the first time. My neighbor Shorty (God rest his soul), his stories could be a whole nother book.

I came home from work one day; my wife said, "Shorty needs a new tractor," and I had to ask why. Lori stated, "He goes one or two rounds picking corn and goes to the store for gas." I laughed and laughed, finally explaining that the tractor didn't need gas, he did!

Talking about Shorty, he told me about a watermelon patch he and Willis (who owned the Lovell store and is my great-uncle; we're all related in Lovell) had in the '30s. Kids kept taking watermelons out of it, and they wanted it to stop, so they devised a plan. Shorty was going to be out there with the kids in the patch when Willis would sneak up and fire his shotgun over their heads. Shorty had ketchup packs in his pocket, and he squashed them when Willis fired the gun, yelling, "*I got shot*!" (I guess it stopped the kids from stealing watermelons!)

Talking about Uncle Willis (he could most definitely be another book), he took a guy down to a house where he kept softener salt for the store. When they got there, a nice old lady came to the door. Willis started cussing and swearing up one side and down the other at her. The guy with him turned red, not knowing what to do. I guess about a week later Willis explained to him that the lady was deaf (very mean but funny).

If you haven't noticed, one story seems to ramble on into another and another!

Shorty told me about how my dad and uncle, when they were ten or so, used to break into the garage across the road from me. They tunneled under the garage to play pool. Bob, who used to live there, saw them one day digging their way in; so he snuck up behind them and fired his shotgun in the air. (I guess they had to change their pants!)

* * *

My first camping episodes were in my neighbor Shorty's woods. I was probably seventeen or eighteen. I went to the house. Dad and I switched vehicles, and he went back; my buddy thought it was me, so he started throwing beer cans at the truck. Dad said when he got out, Tim turned pale, almost passing out! Dad knew we drank a lot back there; he just told us not to leave. (I don't know if Mom knew, but she does now!)

In another such camping trip, one of many, we walked down to the corner of the road, and two of us were twisting a stop sign off (can't explain why other than alcohol). One guy shoved us out of the way, saying he could do it better just as the sign spun back and cut his head open. There was an old swing set at the campgrounds; we said he hit his head on it chasing a Frisbee. (We always thought we buffaloed our parents, but they probably knew better!)

Alcohol and Fireworks—A Very Good Mixture!

In yet another camping trip, we got into fireworks. One kid, trouble always followed him (I could easily write a book on the trouble he got into and still does to this day); he was throwing fireworks at us when somebody got mad and threw one at him. He went to brush it away, but he shoved it down his pocket, where he had a bunch more. They all went off; he started jumping around, screaming, yelling, and then crying. We thought Jim was hurt bad; we finally got him to calm down. Here he was OK but was upset because the fireworks blew a hole in his underwear, and he thought his mom would be mad. (Like I said, alcohol.)

Alcohol, Camping, and Fireworks Don't Mix!
(No kidding.)

We were again camping back in Shorty's woods when somebody got the bright idea to throw a whole brick of firecrackers (which were better than what you can buy today) into the fire. Not only did we have a sheriff driving around trying to figure out what happened, but we ended up with holes on top of our tents from the hot ashes. And the ashes didn't do the car's paint any good either!

Another time, somebody (same guys) got another bright idea—to throw a whole gross of bottle rockets into the fire. We were all diving for cover. I don't know how we didn't get injured; I had a bottle rocket glance off my head! Couple of chairs got ruined in that episode. (Bright ideas, Rick and Al, and you didn't even have any alcohol.)

What a First Day

My eighteenth birthday was my first day of college at Toledo University. My buddies bet me I couldn't drink sixteen beers in one hour and walk up to my room. Well, I did, putting away seventeen; the problem was when I got up there and on the top bunk, I started throwing up all over the wall. It went over real well with my roommate, who hated alcohol to start with! (Almost my first and last day with him.)

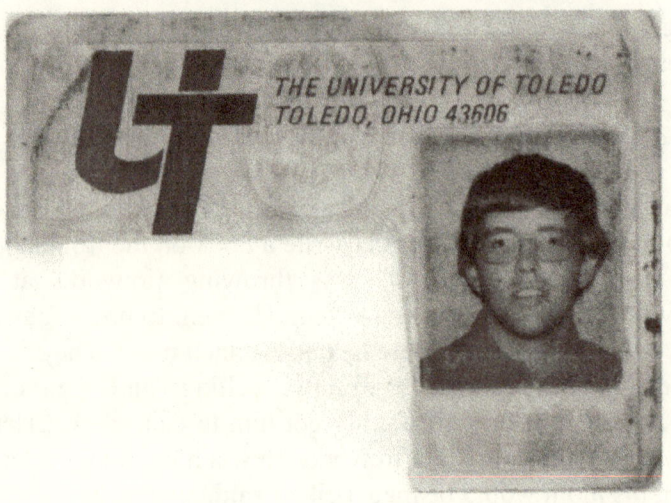

Real Chick Magnet

I stayed away (for the most part) from pot in college; it seemed like everybody was doing it though. One very funny story happened with this very straight kid who had strict parents; he got into pot. He was smoking it through a water bong, I guess for some time, without changing the water. His parents were coming the next day, and he dropped the water bong, spilling pot all over his carpet.

It smelled like a pot factory, so he went and rented a shampooer. He shampooed and shampooed some more, I counted at least five times, and the smell was probably gone; but people down the hall kept coming, telling him it still stunk like pot. Then we told people from the floor below to come up, and they did, telling him they could smell it down there; so he shampooed some more! Finally, we told him it was OK after around a dozen or so cleanings! (Had to have the cleanest carpet on campus, and his parents probably really thought something was up!)

RURAL HUMOR

* * *

Rural areas are big on their festivals; we have 'em for pumpkins, bratwurst, popcorn, change of season—you name it, we've got it. I always thought the church festivals with beer and gambling were different. I've been to Vegas many times, but it just seemed a strange activity in a church parking lot. About forty miles east of me, they have one of the strangest festivals I've heard of. In the little town of Tiro, Ohio, is one called the Tiro Testicle Festival! (No kidding.)

(E-mail if you have any interesting festival stories.)

That last festival reminds me of the farmer who went to Spain and fell in love with the bullfights. Back in America, he fell on hard times and got into financial trouble. He decided to go with what he loved and have Sunday afternoon bullfights. He started a little restaurant there too, with the Monday special being the testicles from the bullfight.

A businessman from the big city came every Monday like clockwork, paying big money for the meal. He had a huge appetite, and he liked the special because they were humongous. One week, the businessman came as usual on Monday; but when they brought the special out, they were very small! He asked what happened. The farmer replied, "Did you read the sign on the door?"

"No," was the reply, "what did it say?"

"Bullfighter needed. Sometimes the bull WINS!"

(I was told this was a true story; my guess is it's the ultimate *bull* story!)

Jarts Champion

We were playing yard jarts (the ones that are outlawed now), and you need to end up on 21; you can't go over. My father-in-law was at 21, so he said, "I will show you how to throw off." Boy, did he ever—right through the garage window. (Kids all said, "Good thing it wasn't us.")

Cold Shatters?

I am writing this on January 15, 2009, and the temperature is twelve below zero, dropping fast and heading for a possible all-time-record low of twenty-plus below. (So much for Al Gore's global warming.) The cold reminds me of yet another story. (Also, I need to bring in my brass monkey.)

We had borrowed the shop station wagon to drive to our high school basketball game. On the way home, we drove the back roads with a case (or two) of beer. One guy went to throw an empty bottle out the window, but the window was only half rolled down; he caught the top and shattered it. We drove home very cold because it was twelve below that night. I put the station wagon back in the parking lot, not saying a word. The next day, I heard them say in the shop, "It was so cold last night the window in the station wagon just shattered!" Here I go telling on myself again! (Hope enough time has passed on this one!)

Even Rural Churches Are Different!

All the young (and old) farmers that I've talked to were heading to church Thursday night; seemed odd because that's not a usual night, and a lot of them didn't belong to that church anyway. Then somebody showed me the church bulletin. Quote: "Ladies of the church have cast off clothes. They can be viewed Thursday night at 7:30." (What the heck. I figured they had something crossed up, but thought I better go just to make sure!) Note: This was from an actual church bulletin, but I can't remember where.

Even Courting Is Different in the Country!

The first time I remember seeing my future wife, I was at a barn playing basketball; the upstairs of it had the old junior high gym floor. Lori was a tenth grader, and I was just out of school. She was driving on the lane in somebody else's pickup truck with five kids in the back end, going too fast, and she almost rolled it. The owner of the barn was standing beside me, and we were wondering who that idiot driving was! (Little did I know it was my future wife.)

The next time I saw her, we were playing tackle football, of all things, with a steel fence as the back of the end zone. I pushed her so she wouldn't catch a pass; and Lori landed on the fence, cutting her arm wide open, requiring stitches. (Very impressive.)

On our first formal date, she was going out with my best friend, and I was going out with her best friend. Very normal! She finally asked me out behind his back, and my best friend has been thanking me ever since. (Just kidding, honey.) It's actually all worked out great as we are all happily married.

Even Rural Hospitals Are Different!

I saw an anesthesiologist's business card; it read, "Come sleep with me. I am the best."

One septic tanker's truck read, "Yesterday's meals on wheels."

Yes, Rural Humor Is Different!

One farmer's sign on his fence said, "Dog food is expensive. Come on in." I stayed in my truck!

A rural muffler shop had a sign: "No need to call. We hear you coming!"

One restaurant in the middle of nowhere had a sign that read, "Hungry? Come on in. Our service will get you fed up!"

One rural radiator shop had a sign: "We invite you to take a leak!" I had had three cups of coffee, and I took that sign literally!

One younger, good-looking male plumber's (didn't have plumber's crack) business card read, "Sleeping with a drip? Call me." You would be surprised how many farmers' wives called!

One electrician had a sign on *her* truck: "Let me remove your shorts!" She got every farmer's business! Rumor was some didn't even have electrical problems!

One funeral house on the edge of a small town had a sign that read, "Slow down. We'll wait."

Sign in one rural tire shop read, "Let us host your next blowout!"

Even Rural Government Is Different!

A mayor was giving his farewell speech when one old farmwife stood up and said, "Your successor won't be as good as you." Afterward, he saw her and told her that wouldn't be true. "It will be," was her reply.

"How do you know?" the mayor said.

"Because I have known seven new mayors, each one worse than the one before I gripped." (Sounds like they have a lot in common with big cities.)

Even Investment Advice Is Different in the Country!

I overheard a young farmer asking an older farmer, "What's the best way to make a small fortune?" The old farmer thought for a moment, then said, "These days, I guess start with a big one!" (Or, author's advice, marry a rich widow.)

Men, however, are the same in the country as in the city (my wife would say, "Pigs"). Our local propane company hired a young gal to paint their tanks. Of course, some were close to the road; after several near wrecks, the local sheriff told her to wear more clothes! (My only regret was not seeing her.)

Words of Wisdom, Quotes, and Sayings

Here are some of the most common sayings I've heard from farmers and others.

"It was two hundred bushels of corn." (This was at the coffee shop.)
"It was one hundred bushels of corn." (Same field, only at the account or landlord's office!)

"Nothing runs like a Deere."
(Unless you own a John Deere, and it broke down!)

"My neighbor is always running around like a chicken with his head cut off." (Translation: My neighbor has no plans in life. [I guess!])

* * *

On any of these translations, if you have a better one, e-mail me.
"I could be all wet!" (My wife says, "No doubt!")
One old farmer used to tell me, "Life's a bitch, then you die!" (Sounds more like an attorney's outlook on life than a farmer's.)
"Death and taxes—the only sure thing in life." (No kidding!)

* * *

Farmers have a lot of sayings for farting too. (And they practice them too!)

"Like a fart in the wind." (Translation: very insignificant. Though I know a guy that can stop a 30 mph wind—Tedd.)
"Like a fart in a skillet." (Can't sit still. Like my grandson!)

Warning: taken literally could be dangerous!

* * *

"Should've planted deeper."
"Should've planted shallower." (Talking about the same field.)

"It's too dry."
"It's too wet." (One day and nine inches of rain after the first statement!)

One shrewd old farmer, when I would try to deal with him, would say, "Let's talk turkey." (I usually lost mine too!)

Set in his ways was this old farmer: "I don't need a computer. I got my instincts." (Feeling of a lot of older farmers.)

Smart Farmer!

Always told me he stayed in the field longer on his wife's certain time of the month.

He told me also what PMS maybe stands for (potential murder suspect). Gives me an idea to put women with PMS on border patrol; our borders would be secure by the end of the period! (If that was the first thing an illegal met, he would head straight back over the border.)

One older farmer always told me, "Money isn't everything." (Yeah, but it sure helps!)

Several farmers always said, "Farming—it's a matter of life or death." (Hopefully, it's not that severe!)

One farmer said on planting on time, "Just once I would like to do it right." (I think that's what he was talking about anyway.)

One stingy farmer (actually, more than one, but one in particular) always told me, "I'll make you an offer you can't refuse." (I usually could!)

Not the most honest farmer told me more than once, "You get what you deserve." I never knew for sure if he was taking about crop yields, his wife, or life in general. (He didn't deserve much though!)

One farmer, third or fourth generation, told me, "Failure is not an option." (I think he meant on keeping the family farm going.)

Most farmers do have pride in keeping family farms going. (There are some, though, that don't give a damn and would sell for a buck.)

One day a young farmer told me, "I have failed as many times as I have succeeded." (Sounds more like a gambler.)

As I wrote that last line down, it came to me that farming is the ultimate gamble! (You gamble your crops will grow! You gamble on the weather! You gamble that if you do get a crop, you will get a good price!)

I used to wonder what the farmer meant when he told me, "Who said farmers are logical?" He was talking about taking up farming, I think. (After that thought on gambling, I understand his mindset.)

This farmer told me a statement you've probably heard: "Keep your friends close, but your enemies closer." I gathered he was talking about government entities. (I hope not his tractor salesman!)

A cattle farmer told me this: "Look out for number 1, but don't step in number 2!" (Good idea!)

One rather sour old farmer told me this: "I saw my whole life flash before my eyes. It was a bitch, then I died." (Great outlook!)

Farmer told me one everybody's heard: "An apple a day will keep the doctor away." I wasn't sure why the farmer told me that till he showed me he makes apple wine! (I now agree!)

A kind of different farmer told me, "I make more money between the rows." He was referring to illegal crops. I think he was just kidding. (Maybe I better check though!)

I heard farmers say this many times: "Made too much money." (Translation: I got to pay taxes, darn it.) Believe me, farmers hate to pay taxes! They will pay for seed, fertilizer, or anything they can for the following year to avoid taxes. (Hopefully, buy some equipment too from me.)

I believe the farmer that told me this one was talking about yields when he said, "By god, wait till next year." Or the more I think about it, he may have meant avoiding taxes! (Or it was the coach of the Cleveland Indians. Or Browns!)

Many a farmer, after getting back from their accountant, has told me this: "I need to write you a check on that piece of equipment on the end of the year business." (This is February 1, by the way! That whole tax thing!)

The farmer that told me this was not a baseball fan: "It's not over till it's over." He was the most pessimistic farmer I knew. He would have great-looking crops; I would stop to see him about equipment, and he would think something was going to happen to the crops—hailstorm, flood, an act of God, or whatever! (More I think about it now, he probably says those things for an excuse not to buy!)

Another farmer would say the same thing this way, and he was not a sports fan either! "It's not over till the fat lady sings." (I didn't have the heart to tell him when the time comes that his wife could do the honor!)

My good neighbor told me this one: "You can balance an egg on end during the equinox." (Hint from the author: I tried it; superglue helps!) He was talking about the one from spring to summer, I believe.

I saw my neighbor putting extra wood on his back porch, so I stopped to ask him what was going on. He said, "I saw a dark Willy worm, which means a cold winter." So I started helping him throw more wood on the porch. (After all, I saw that same Willy worm.)

Another commonly used phrase in the country is, "Frost on the pumpkin. Time for . . ." (Whoops, I can't finish that one.)

* * *

Today, March 7, 2009, a farmer came in the shop and declared, "Spring is here!" A robin just showed up in his backyard. I said, "What if winter comes back?" His reply? "Probably a stupid robin!" (Or the robin listens to the same mixed-up weatherman I do.)

In the country, they say it's six weeks till a frost after you hear the first locust. I heard city folks have a different twist to this; they say it's six weeks till a frost after JC Penney puts out its winter coats. (Honestly, I don't know which is correct!)

Several farmers would say this: "When hell freezes over." Their translation: will never happen. Hope they weren't referring to buying equipment off me! (If it did happen, I would snowmobile there too!)

One good old farm customer who was very religious surprised me on this one. He had just sold ground to the government for the eleventh time because he lived at the corner of US 30 and 1-75. I asked him how he got such a good deal from the government; he said, "You need to find a lawyer that is a real scheister, one you wouldn't even want as a friend!" (Later, I thought he didn't eliminate many.)

Grandma told me this one thirty or forty years ago: "A watched pot never boils." (I tried this, though, and it did boil; now I am depressed, thinking my grandma was a liar.) Here's a 2008 update to this saying: "A watched e-mail never pops." (This was a quote from a writer waiting to see who Obama's running mate would be. That was a waste of time!)

Farmers' Three Biggest Lies

1. It really was two hundred bushels of corn!
2. My diesel truck really does get twenty-five miles per gallon!
3. I really was just helping that sheep over the fence! (Just kidding. I hope.)

* * *

One old farmer always said, "Don't take any wooden nickels." (Translation: don't take anything worthless.) Another tip from the author: wooden nickels were used in the 1800s; if you get a chance, take it!

This farmer would say,

- "I will do whatever till the cows come home!"
- "I will do whatever till pigs fly!"
- "I will do whatever till the darn equipment salesman leaves me alone!"(I hope he wasn't talking about me!)

You've probably heard this, and I have from many farmers: "Get the hell out of Dodge." (Never been to Dodge, but it sure sounds like a place to stay out of.)

Another common saying I've heard from farmers and Dorothy on *The Wizard of Oz* is, "We're not in Kansas anymore." (Trust me, I've been in Kansas, and I wouldn't worry about not being there.)

Another common phrase farmers use a lot is, "When in Rome, do like the Romans." (Again, never been to Rome, but I guess it means do like the locals. Unless they jump off a bridge!) Farmers love to say, "They live in a little Podunk town." (I have no idea if that is good or bad.)

I found out Podunk came from a tribe of Indians that disappeared in Connecticut. So people started saying, "Where are the Podunk's?" It became a joke to describe a place that was too remote to find or too small to find. (I thought I should make this book informative as well as funny!)

This is what lot of farmers say when buying something: "I paid through the nose." (Sounds painful.) Being informative (again!), "paying through the nose" came from the Swedish in the fourteenth century; they used to make them pay taxes by the number of noses in the household!

(Sounds like government, doesn't it?)

More Lesser-Known Facts!

There are seven hundred thousand physicians in the United States who cause 120,000 accidental deaths per year, according to the United States Department of Health and Human Services. There are eighty million gun owners causing only 1,500 accidental deaths! So statistically, doctors are nine times more dangerous than gun owners.

That means the old farmer riding around with his shotgun in the back window is no danger, but the doctor in town sure is, let alone lawyers. Out of concern for the public, I left their statistics out for fear it would cause people to panic and go see their doctor! (Always concerned for you.)

* * *

This is a favorite saying at the coffee shop by rural folks: "It came straight from the horse's mouth." (If true, it better be cleaned first!)

Another horsey statement: "Don't look a gift horse in the mouth." (Translation: Take it and shut up!)

Farmers are always saying, "I got it planted by the skin of my teeth." I know it means "just in time." (But where is the skin of your teeth?)

Once again, I feel the need to be informative. "Skin of your teeth" came from the Bible, Job 19:20. If I keep this up, and I will not know whether to have this book in the intelligence department or the comedy section. (Wife says, "Don't worry.")

Lots of rural folks say they live by the golden rule, and generally they do. (I've always hoped real gold was involved though!)

Farmers like to say, "They're Even Steven." I guess it means, "We're back to square one." (Though I have never met Even Steven!)

Another of their favorite sayings is, "It's time to face the music." I think most meant time to pay their end-of-the-season bills. (Though some meant it was time to tell their wife they bought a new tractor!)

Common saying farmers like to use is, "It's all hunky dory." I guess they mean "under control." (Till they get in the house and tell their wife about the new tractor!)

Another familiar quote they like is, "Time to throw in the towel." (While most farmers are talking about their crops, some are talking about taking back that *new* tractor before the wife finds out!)

On planting on time, lots of farmers say this: "I got it in just in the nick of time." Farm boys said something similar, but I think it had a whole different meaning! "I got it out just in the nick of time." (Hopefully.)

* * *

Lots of changes in farming like bigger and bigger equipment and where they get their information (older farmers from the barbershop or the coffee shop while the younger ones use the Internet [the coffee shop is probably more truthful]).

Farmers' crop rotation also has changed from CBL to CBF (from corn, beans, and livestock to corn, beans, and Florida)!

A lot of this change has to do with aging farm population.

Older farmers are always telling how much harder they had it. In most cases, they did like milking cows by hand, no cab tractors, horses, no tractors at all, and so forth.

The best one I heard was when an old farmer told me, quote, "I walked three miles to and from school, and both ways were uphill!" (I always wondered why he didn't walk the other way so both ways would have been downhill!)

Farmers Are Tight!

I know several farmers too tight to get married; plus they would have to leave home, *or* they knew life ended when you get married! (Just kidding, Lori.)

The old saying, "Keeping up with the Joneses," has real meaning in the farm community. I knew more than one farmer who wouldn't buy a tractor or even a pickup truck till his neighbor did. That way, he could buy a bigger or better one!

That's true in more than the farm community:

* Gun with a bigger scope
* Fishing pole with a bigger reel
* Wife with bigger—oops! (Just kidding again, honey.)

* * *

My old friend that rides around with me on sales calls told me this one: "A January thaw brings a May freeze." Another way of putting it would be, "A January day that doesn't go below thirty-two, the same day in May (or close) will be way below normal." (Don says he's checked it out. I need to.)

When It Comes to Rain, Farmers Have A Lot of Sayings!

One you've probably heard, and the rural community says it a lot, is, "It's raining cats and dogs." (Seems it would be messy!)

Couple of farmers and my dad were always saying this one: "Raining like a cow peeing on a flat rock!" (I have no idea, and I am not going to try to guess!)

One farmer told me this one several times during a drought: "It will rain again." (Translation: no kidding.)

Another one I hear from people that bale hay is, "Every time I mow down hay, it rains!" (Translation: damn poor planning!)

One farmer always said, "It's rained so many days, I was getting ready to build an ark!" (I never could figure out if he was religious or telling a joke!)

Here's another one my old friend (I better quit calling him old!) told me: "River puts ice on the bank, it will come back to get it before spring." (Sounds like a fancy way of saying, "It was a damn wet winter" to me.)

"Rain on Easter Sunday means rain the next seven Sundays!" (Translation: hope you don't have outdoor plans the next few weekends.)

Seen this myself many times: "Bubbles in the puddles during rain means more coming." (Kind of even rhymes too.)

I've told you I only read a couple of books in my life; the Bible is one. I would like to get around to reading from cover to cover. (If anybody knows the best version to read, give me a shout.)

I heard farmers and rural meteorologist say this about floods: "It was a fifty-year flood," or "It was a two-hundred-year event," or "It was a flood of biblical proportion." I figured if I read the Bible from cover to cover, I would know the answer to the last one. My best guess though is, "It's time to start building an *ark* (or bend over and grab your ankles)!"

One older farmer used to tell me this one: "You're beating a dead horse." (Translation: move on with your life! Hope PETA didn't hear this one!)

Most of you have probably heard this one that farmers use a lot: "I will kill two birds with one stone," but you probably didn't hear what one farmer's daughter (blonde) said. "Isn't that cruel?" (She is probably a college grad and a member of PETA!)

Speaking of animal agencies, I got a good true story. My relation dressed up as a clown and brought his goat (Blaze) to the Wyandot County Fair. It would pull a cart and blow up balloons; everybody over three knew what was going on, except for one animal group. Clareon, the clown, told me they actually filed papers against him for cruelty to the goat for making it blow up all the balloons. He said they just shook their heads and walked away when he showed them the compressor on his waist with the hose running down his sleeve! (Get a real life!)

Finally, it was on March 15, 2009, at a church dart ball tournament when I was told this one: "When you hear your first bullfrog [not the Budweiser one], there will be three more frost."

(I would like to hear that first bullfrog about January 15!)

Any good sayings or better explanations than what I gave, give me an e-mail. (Thanks, and I think you will get a laugh out of the next chapter.)

Chapter 3

Rural Humor
Funny Stories About Rural America
(some true, some partially true,
Some just pure *bull!*)

But remember, this is all in the spirit of fun.
The world is too serious. Read and enjoy!

I have been writing this chapter for well over thirty years, and since I don't read books, my stories come from farmers, meetings, lunches at meetings, bars after meetings, campfire meetings, and countless other places (not the Internet)!

My use for the internet

I hope you enjoy!

Overoptimistic Farmer!

One of the earliest stories about a farmer I heard was about the one who was out plowing, and he turned up a genie's lantern. The genie came out, thanking the farmer for releasing him and said he would grant him three wishes.

When the genie asked for the first wish, the farmer said, "I have farmed my whole life and would like to sell twenty-dollar beans. Fine. Done. One month from that day, the genie was back for a second wish; the farmer stated he would like all his bills and mortgage paid. Fine. Done. One month later, the genie was back, asking him for his third wish. Farmer replied, "I would like to sell twenty-dollar beans." The genie, puzzled, said, "I already granted you that." The farmer replied, quote, "I know, but I didn't sell them. I thought they would go *higher*!" (Sound like any farmers you know?)

* * *

If my donkey jumps the fence and eats your rooster's two feet, what would you have?

Answer: two feet of your [rooster's other name] up my [donkey's other name]. (Don't think too hard!)

Facts About Burials You May Not Know!

While seven feet or so is normal burial depth, lawyers get buried at twelve feet and farmers at two feet. Why, you might ask. Well, lawyers, they found out, really are nice deep down. Farmers, meanwhile, still need to get one arm out for handouts! (Just kidding. I think.)

It was a farmer that was divorced that told me this one (so I figured her lawyer took him to the cleaners): Do you know the difference between a dead lawyer and a dead skunk in the middle of the road? There were skid marks before the skunk!

Do you know *how* to tell when a lawyer (or used tractor salesman) is lying? Their lips move!

Job Offer

A former farmer, suicidal over being out of work, calls the suicide hotline. When they found out he was suicidal and could drive a truck, they got all excited and offered him a job. (On the bad part, the line was being manned in Iraq.)

Farmers like to recycle (they're tight). Take the farmer that turned his old dishwasher into a snow blower. How, you might ask? He gave the — itch a shovel. (I think that marriage ended with a shovel over the head.)

* * *

Farmers' wives can get mad. (In many cases, like the last one, the farmers deserve it.)

One farmer's wife, questioned by the sheriff, was asked why she ran over her husband twice with the tractor.

She replied, "It was an accident."
Sheriff replies, "Both times?"
"Oh no," she replies, "*just the second time!*"

* * *

Two CIA agents hold tryouts in a rural community, putting an ad in the paper stating they are looking for people who can follow orders to a tee. Two farmers and one farmwife show up.

First the CIA agents send one of the farmers in the room, give him a gun, and tell him to shoot whatever is in there. It's his wife; he can't. He comes out, hands them his gun. CIA agents tell him they don't want him.

They send the other farmer into the room, tell him to shoot whatever is in there. He can't. It's his daughter in there; he comes out, gives back the gun. They reply, "We can't use you."

Finally it's the farmwife's turn; they give her the gun and send her into the room and tell her to shoot whatever is in there. They hear *pop, pop, pop*, then horrible screaming; the two CIA guys look at each other, puzzled. The wife comes out, blood all over her, hands them the gun, and says, "*Your gun only shoots blanks, so I had to beat my husband to death with it!*" (Tip: don't cross her.)

* * *

Farmer's wife calls 911, screaming, "I think my husband's dead! I think he's dead!" The 911 operator says, "Calm down. Go check. *Make sure* your husband's not breathing." What the 911 operator hears next is, "Oh shit," and a gunshot. Then the wife gets back on the phone and says, "What next?" (Smart wife or dumb wife?)

* * *

A farmer, along with his wife, goes to the bank; and they are standing in line when it gets robbed.

The robber shoots the teller dead, then he turns to the guy behind him to see if he saw what happened. The guy says he did, so the robber shoots him dead. Next in line is the farmer's wife. The robber says, "Did you see what happened?" "Oh no," is the reply, "but my husband *behind* me sure did!" (Clever!)

* * *

One farmer's wife (blonde) took her dog to the vet and saw her friend from town was there and asked her why she was there.

The friend said her dog was old and needed to be put to sleep. "Why are you here?" she asked.

The farmer's wife replied, "Well, I was getting out of the shower when I dropped my towel, so I bent over, and the dog tried to mount me."

"So you're having it put to sleep?"

"Oh no, no, I'm having his toenails trimmed!"

(Oh my, my.)

Note from author: Farmers would never go to the vet and pay to have a dog put to sleep; they would shoot it first.

* * *

A nice-looking (hot!) farmer's wife (*blonde*) goes to the dentist to have a tooth pulled.

She complains to him, saying, "I'd rather have a baby than have this tooth pulled."

The dentist says, "Make up your mind. It makes a difference how I adjust this chair!"

(I never did hear what she decided!)

Thoughtful Farmer?

Farmer is out working on his ground and accidentally runs over a mother skunk and her babies, killing the mother. He is a real animal lover, and he doesn't want to see the babies die, so he takes them home. The farmer sees they are cold. He thinks and thinks; finally, he takes and puts them under the covers with his wife, who is already asleep. This seems to warm them right up. The next day, the farmer gets out of bed ahead of his wife, taking off with the skunks for the neighbor's house to ask him what to do; the neighbor is a vet (of WWII). The farmer tells the vet that he had put them in bed with his wife, and it seemed to warm them right up. The vet goes, "My god, what about the smell?" And the farmer replies, quote, "*They didn't seem to mind!*" (Pee-yew!)

* * *

A younger farmer was in deep trouble. His wife left him, dog turned on him, they repossessed his combine and were foreclosing on his farm; so he chucked it all, taking off for Alaska. He moved out in the middle of nowhere (Podunk) and had not seen anybody for six months or so.

Finally getting lonely, he went over the mountain to see if there were any neighbors; sure enough, there was a cabin with smoke coming out of it. So he knocked on the door, and a guy opened it up.

The former farmer introduced himself, telling the guy he was his neighbor over the hill. The guy said he was having a party next Friday and asked him if he would like to come.

"Sure," the former farmer replied quickly. "I've been lonely and would like to get out." And he turned to leave.

The guy called him back and said, "There will be a lot of drinking, hope you don't mind."

The farmer said he didn't and again left. The guy yelled, "Come back!" again, so he did. The neighbor winked, telling him, "There will be a lot of playing around going on, hope it won't bother you."

The farmer said, "I still want to get out, that's OK," and started to leave. This time he turned around himself, coming back. He asked the guy, "By the way, what would I wear to a party like this?"

And the guy said, quote, "I don't care, it's only going to be you and me!" (Suppose he went. Even farmers get fooled!)

* * *

Farmer goes to town, gets a new rooster, brings it home, and turns it loose with the chickens. The old rooster comes up to the new rooster and says he just wants two hens.

"Nope, I'm taking them all."

He asks again, for only one this time.

"Nope," says the new rooster. "I'm taking them all."

Finally the old rooster says, "Let's race around the henhouse. I win, I get one hen."

The new rooster laughs because the old rooster can hardly walk. The old rooster says, "If you think it will be so easy, give me a half a lap lead."

"Fine."

The race is on. The farmer hears all the commotion, grabs his gun because he thinks there might be a fox in the henhouse. What he sees is the new rooster almost ready to catch the old one; only one lap into the race, and the farmer shoots the new rooster dead.

Farmer walks back into the house, sets down his gun, tells his wife, quote, "Can't get any good roosters from town. That's the third *queer* one I've had to shoot this week!" (Smart old rooster.)

Cheaper Is Not Always Better

Another farmer goes to town to buy a rooster. The rooster salesman recommends one for forty-five dollars.

"Too much," says the farmer. "How about this one over there for ten bucks?"

"Don't buy it," says the rooster salesman. "Get this one over here for thirty dollars."

"No, I like the one for ten bucks." The salesman says, "It's promiscuous." "It is what?" asks the farmer.

"Overhorny," says the rooster salesman. "That's what I want," says the farmer. "OK, but I warned you."

So the farmer takes it home, turns it loose with the chickens, and goes to bed. The next day, the farmer goes into the barn; all the hens are dead. He goes to the hog barn; the rooster got to all of them, and the horses too!

He looks around; there lies the rooster, looking dead, in the middle of the field with a buzzard circling overhead. The farmer thinks, *Well, he fixed himself*, and starts to walk out that way; but the rooster motions for him to stop, signaling the buzzard is about to land.

(Wonder if he got into the farmer's Viagra?) E-mail me with your best chicken joke.

Cheaper Is Definitely Not Better

The poor young farmer went to the chicken ranch (whorehouse), asked what the special was; the madam said it was Susie for $49.99 in room 312.

The poor farmer sobbed and said, "I don't have that much," and turned around to leave; but the madam, feeling sorry, stopped him and asked him how much he had. "Fifteen," replied the farmer.

Well, she thought. "Go upstairs, second floor, third door on the left. There is a chicken."

He said, "You got to be kidding, but if that's all you got for fifteen bucks, I will take it."

The poor farmer came back a week later, asked what the special was.

"Betty Lou, third floor, twenty-five bucks," she replied.

He said, "I only got ten bucks this week," and turned to leave.

The madam, feeling sorry, stopped him again and said, "You can go upstairs, second floor, second door on the left, and watch people through a two-way mirror."

He was desperate, so he went upstairs and sat down in the room. Took one look. Two airline stewards were chasing each other around. (Just kidding, stewards. I knew one once that wasn't gay. I think.) The poor farmer said, "This is disgusting. I can't watch this."

The guy beside him said, "This is nothing. Should have been here last week. Some guy was chasing a chicken!" (No pictures needed!)

Stranded Farmer

A farmer got stranded on a deserted island after a shipwreck; he had floated there on a life raft by himself and had been there for about six months. (So he hasn't actually missed any work yet.) One day, he turned around, and a gorgeous blonde was standing there in a trench coat.

She says, "I got three things for you. One, you probably miss coffee with your buddies at the coffee shop, don't you?"

"Why, yes," replied the farmer. The blonde pulls out a thermos of coffee.

"Two, you probably miss checking commodity prices on the computer."

"Why, yes," was the reply again. She pulls out a laptop for him.

"Three, you miss playing around, don't you?" and she starts to open the trench coat.

The farmer says, "You're kidding me. You got a set of golf clubs in there too?"

(Really out to sea.)

Farmer and His Tools

While a normal farmer gets by with duct tape and baling twine, an advanced farmer has pliers. But your really advanced farmer has a Leatherman (imitation, of course).

* * *

Not to say some farmers whine, but the funniest part of this is that, the farmer who told me this was the biggest whiner of all. The difference between a 747 and a farmer is that the 747 quits whining when it touches down in Florida. (Farmers, if you don't like it, substitute "farmer" with "mother-in-law" or just get over it.)

* * *

Not to say farmers are cheap, but do you know why they don't wear tennis shoes? Seed corn companies don't give them away! (Or farm equipment dealers.)

Sick Farm Jokes

Farmer gets his left arm cut off in a combine. No problem! (He's all right.) How does a farm wife punish her blind daughter? (Rearranges the furniture.)

Worst thing about eating vegetables on the farm? (Getting Granny out of the wheelchair!)

Poor old farmer sends wife out to the corner to earn money (as a hooker). She comes in with $20.25. Farmer says, "What SOB gave you twenty-five cents?" She replies, "All of them." (Oh my!)

Do you know what a farm boy does in West Virginia when he wants a date? He goes to his family reunion! (Actually, that's what a University of Michigan football player does too!)

Do you know a backwoods farmer's definition of "relative humidity"? When sweat drips down his back and runs down his sister-in-law's side. Think about it! (And you'll never think of *relative* humidity in the same way!)

Two good old farmers are sitting on the porch. One farmer asks, "If I mess around with your wife, and she gets pregnant, would we be related?"

"She's your sister. You need to ask her!" (OK!)

One farmer asked me this one. Do you know the definition of one American leader (liter)?

Answer: what Monica Lewinsky's mouth holds! (I will not explain!)

Did you read what the farm girl (I think from West Virginia or southern Ohio, same difference) asked Dear Abby? "I am almost fourteen and still a virgin. Do you think my brothers are gay?" (I would like to see her response to that one!)

Hope these weren't too sick. You have any good sick jokes, e-mail me.

City Slicker vs. Farmer

A city slicker thinks his glass is half empty; a farmer drinks it!

A city slicker thinks cereal comes from a box; farmers grow it!

A city slicker thinks steaks come from Kroger's; farmers raise them!

A city slicker thinks Bambi (deer) is cute; farmers shoot them (for food, eating their crops, and being a danger to their pickup and your car)!

A city slicker thinks New York, Chicago, and Los Angeles are the greatest while a farmer (and me) thinks, "What the hell is this traffic?"(And can't wait to get back home.)

A city slicker loves his indoor animals; farmers knows where they belong! (In the barn!)

A city slicker loves to party till 4:00 a.m.; farmers love to get up at 4:00 a.m. (Not necessary funny but true.)

A city slicker thinks a beautiful woman's ears are for listening to his great wisdom, but even a country boy knows what they really good for—to hold on to! (I won't explain this further!)

City Slicker and the Farmer
(even had run-ins at the turn of the century)

Take the traveling salesman from the city in his horse-drawn carriage. He was pushing it too hard on a hot day, and the horse fell over dead, right in front of a farmer's place with horses for sale. So he went to talk to the farmer about buying a replacement, and the farmer said, "Take this one, he's only three hundred bucks."

"Too much," said the tight salesman as he pointed to one over there and asked how much.

"One hundred," replied the farmer. "But he doesn't look too good."

"Looks good to me." So he paid the farmer. The salesman, in a hurry, hooked the horse up to his carriage and took off, looking at his notes, not paying attention to the road (kind of like cell phones today), he ran off a curve right into a tree. He flew off, ending up face-to-face with the horse. He looked in its eyes, realizing it was blind.

Angry, he took the horse back, demanding his $100 back for selling him a blind horse. The farmer fired back, quote, "I told you he didn't look too good!"

(Forewarned.)

Helpful Farm Boys?

Two farm boys went to town and were eating lunch. The one boy, Leroy, says, "Hey, Ralph, the lady behind us is choking. Should we help her?"

"No, she'll be OK."

But five minutes later, the lady is still coughing. Leroy says again, "We better help her."

Again Ralph says, "No, she'll be OK."

They continue to eat lunch. A few minutes later, Leroy looks over and says, "She's turning blue."

Ralph stands up. "It's time to help."

He goes over beside her, pulls down his pants, and Leroy licks his rear end. The lady, seeing this gets grossed out and throws up, dislodging what was stuck in her throat.

She hugs Ralph and says, "That's the grossest thing I ever seen, but you saved my life. Thank you, thank you, thank you."

Ralph says, "Leroy is the one you really want to thank. He taught me that *hind-lick maneuver!*"

(You'll never think of Heimlich the same way again!) I wonder how much practice it took to learn that?

Helpful Farm Boy?
(again)

Farm boy moves to town and gets a good office job but takes up drinking heavily on the weekends. Almost every Monday, he comes in beaten up from bar fights over the weekend. He announces one Friday that he is giving up drinking and the bar scene; the office people just laugh and don't believe him.

Once again, Monday morning he shows up with two black eyes; the office people say, "I thought you gave up drinking and fighting."

"I did," replies the farm boy.

"Then what about the two black eyes?" asks one co-worker.

"I stayed home all weekend, minding my own business, then I decided to go to church on Sunday. You know how hot and muggy it was? Well, this gorgeous blonde stood up in front of me, and her dress rode way up, showing her bikini underwear. I thought I better help, so I reached up, pulled her dress down, and she punches me right in the left eye."

"Well," says the co-worker, "that explains one eye. How did you get the other black eye?"

Farm boy replies, "I thought she must like it up there, so I put it back!" (Smooth move.)

Farm Boy Helping Another

While building a storage shed, one farm boy noticed the other boy was throwing about half the nails away. He went over and asked him why.

"Well, when I pick them up, a lot of them have the head on the wrong end."

"You idiot, those are for the other side!"

(You can hire them by calling BR-549-IDIOT.)

* * *

Farm boy went to town for some supplies; while he was there, he decided to go to the bar. He told the bartender he had a dumb-city-boy joke to tell. He started to tell it; the bartender stopped him.

"Before you tell it, I better inform you of a few things. That city boy over there was state wrestling champion three years in a row, the one beside him was captain of the football team, the other one, well, he is just plain mean. And all three are attending Michigan University. Do you still want to tell it?"

"Oh no," replies the farm boy. "I got to get back for chores, and I don't have time to explain it three times!"

(Way to go!)

Farm Boy Helping City Boy

A city boy came out hunting, got lucky, and shot a deer. The farm boy is up in his tree stand, and along comes the city boy, dragging the deer.

Trying to be helpful, the farm boy yells down, "If you drag him from the other end, it will pull a lot easier," and he turns around to look for a deer.

A couple of weeks later, he saw that boy in town and asked him if his advice worked.

"Sure did," replied the city boy. "Took me an hour to get to your tree stand. When I took your advice and pulled from the other end, I was back to where I shot it in ten minutes!"

(Genius.)

Farm Boys Can Outsmart City Boys

Take for example the accident that happened just outside of town. A country boy driving his pickup collides with a city boy driving his fancy sports car. The farm boy hops out of his '74 Chevy (not a dent on it, by the way) and goes over to see if the other boy is OK (his sports car is totaled, by the way). He says to the city boy, "You feeling fine?"

"No," he replies. "I don't feel too good."

The farm boy goes to the pickup, comes back, and says, "Here, take a sip of this. It will help." So he did. "Feel better?"

"A little," was the reply.

"Take another sip," so he did.

"I am feeling better," said the city boy. "What is that?"

"Moonshine," replies the farm boy.

"Why don't you take a sip?"

"Oh no," was the farm boy's response. "Not with the sheriff coming!" (Got ya!)

Smart Farm Boy!

Two hot babes from town come out and go skinny-dipping in the farm pond. Farm boy shows up. They yell, "We're not coming out till you leave." He replies, "I am not here to see you, just to feed the alligators!" (Good thinking.)

Slow Farm Boys!

The two of them are walking down the railroad track when one of them kicks a sack, and a head rolls out. The one boy goes, "Oh my, that's our friend George!" The other says, "You idiot, that's not George. He was taller than that!" (Can't argue with thinking like that.)

* * *

The same two farm boys went on their first fishing trip together a couple of states away; they had fished several days with no luck. Finally, late the next-to-last day, they found a really good spot; but just as they got started, a storm came up.

One boy yelled, "Mark the spot while I pull up the anchor!" That night in bed, the one boy woke up and asked the other, "How did you mark the spot?"

He replied, "I put an X in the bottom of the boat!"

"What?" The boy jumped straight up, screaming, "That was really stupid! What if we don't get the same boat?"

(Again, how can argue with thinking like that?)

* * *

The boys this time go on their first hunting trip together out in the Rockies. This being their first trip out west, they are afraid of getting lost and decide to hire a guide (good choice). The guide, after a couple of days, sends them out on their own and tells the farm boys, "If you get lost, fire three shots. I'll come to get you."

They're out hunting all day when one of them says, "We're lost."

With a storm coming, the other pipes up, "We better fire three shots."

So the boy does, but nothing happens, so he fires three more and waits. Finally, the storm's getting closer; the boy again yells, "Fire three more!"

"I can't. I've only got two arrows left!" (*Guide was a slow city boy.*)

The Boys Meet a Tragic End

This time they go on their first hunting trip without a guide. The boys think they've found some fresh tracks and begin to follow when tragedy strikes. In the form of a train!

First and Last

Farm boy goes on his first trip to hunting camp with his friend who is an experienced hunter. His friend takes him out, puts him by a tree, tells him to be quiet. "Don't move unless a deer comes by." About three hours in, the farm boy starts screaming and yelling.

His friend comes running. "What happened?"

"Well, I was standing here, and a bear came up and breathed down my neck.

"That would do it."

"Oh no. I stood still till the bear left." "What happened then?" the friend asks.

"Then a wolf came along, started licking my face." "That would do it."

"Oh no. I stood still till it left." "Then what happened?"

"Then a snake crawled down the tree into my vest." "Oh, I understand now."

"No, no. I stood still till it left. Next was two squirrels. That got me. I'm heading back to camp and drink beer!"

His friend laughed and laughed. "After all that, you let those squirrels get you?"

"Yeah. One crawled up each pant leg and were deciding who's taking which one back to the nest!"

(Close call, man!)

* * *

Did you hear about the three Mexican farm boys detained at the border in Tijuana trying to cross the border illegally? They asked them why. They said, "Because we trying to escape oppressive government, high taxes, and no jobs!" Do you know what they did with those poor boys? They sent them back to California! (Terrible, terrible.)

* * *

Like in the country song "A Country Boy Can Survive," country boys can outhunt and outfish city boys. Take for example the two city boys that came out to the country to ice-fish; they asked the farmer if they could fish on his pond, and he said fine.

They were fishing about one hundred yards apart for several hours and had not caught a fish when out came the farmer's boy. He started fishing between them, pulling up one after another.

Finally, the city boys couldn't take it; they had to come over and find out his secret. They asked him how he was doing so good.

He responded, "Youa needa toa kopa woma."

"What?" they said. "We can't understand."

The farm boy spat the worms out of his mouth and said, "You need to keep the worms warm!"

(I will take his word for it.)

Even Farm Boys Like Jokes

Take the city boy that came out to the country to watch his cousin milk cows. He was watching for a while when the country boy asked him if he wanted to try and milk one. "Sure," was the reply. So the country boy sent him over to the *bull's* stable, and he got something white, but it wasn't milk! (Yuck!)

Country Boys Are Practical

City boy likes a good-looking woman on the back of his Harley. Country boy also likes a pretty-looking woman on the back but, in case of an emergency, would like to know if she can suck-start it! (The Harley, of course.)

Country Girls Are Practical Too!

Take one cold winter night, and a mom asked her daughter why she had on fur-lined panties to go on her date. Quote: "Duh, it's cold, Mom. I want to keep my ankles warm!" (Probably blonde.)

Farm Boys Are Protective Also

Take the two farm boys whose sister had a date with a boy in the city, and she came home crying that Clarence had attacked her. They had never been to town but decided to go looking for him.

The two left for town; pretty soon, the boys were back. When asked why they were back so soon, they replied, quote, "You didn't tell us how big he was."

Their sister asked them what they meant.

"We got almost to town, and the sign on the bridge said 'Clearance 13 ft 6.' We ain't messing with him!"
(Bright boys.)

Even Six-Year-Old Farm Boys Are Kind-hearted

Little Johnny is at church with his parents when the pastor asks if anybody had a prayer request.

Johnny waves his hand, and the pastor asked him what his prayer is.

He replies, "It's for all those twelve-year-old girls on Daddy's computer."

"Why?" asks the pastor.

"Because not one of them can afford any clothes!" (Now Daddy doesn't farm since he is on the run from authorities.)

Even Seven-Year-Old Farm Boys Are Protective

Take the little farm boy standing in line at the grocery store with a weight-challenged (fat) woman in front of them. Her cell phone starts beeping, so the young boy yells, "Mom, run for cover, she's backing up!" (Good boy?)

Even Eight-Year-Old Farm Boys Are Helpful

Eight-year-old Johnny and four-year-old Jimmy Bob (double name, must be from Kentucky) go into the local drugstore and pick up some tampons and go to the counter.

The nice lady there says, "That's nice of you to pick these up for your mother. Most boys won't do that."

Johnny replies, "They're for my little brother."

Puzzled, the lady asks why.

"Well, he's four. We saw on TV that if you use these, you can ride a bike, swim, and he can't do either at this point!" (Very helpful.)

Bad Farm Boys

Two farm boys were on the way to town when they picked up a pretty blonde whose car broke down. The one boy got in the back seat with her, taking her pants off; at the stop sign, she got out and ran off screaming.

The boy says to the other, "Look, I got her pants off."

"Big deal, you dummy, they won't fit you anyway!" (Genius.)

Yet Another Helpful Country Boy

One night, the farm boy sneaks out and goes to town to the bar. He walks in, and just one other guy is there. Over comes the bartender, asking if the boy would help take the other guy home; he needs some help.

The boy says, "Sure, I'd love to, but I am from the country and don't know my way around."

The bartender says, "Come over to the door," and pointed down the street to a house with a light on. "That is where he lives. Take him home, and I will get you a free beer." (Free sounds good to a farm boy and me too!) The phone rings just then, so the bartender goes in the back to answer it.

So the boy grabs the other guy, pulls him off the stool, and the guy falls flat on his face, busting his lip. "Great, he is really wasted," thinks the farm boy. He drags the guy to his car, takes him down the street, drags him up to the door with the light on, tearing his clothes, and knocks on the door. A lady comes to the door.

He says, "Here is your husband. I brought him home from the bar." She is looking all around, puzzled. "What's a wrong?" says the farm boy. "This is your husband?"

"Oh yes," she replies, *"but where is his wheelchair?"*

(Oops!)

First and Last Blind Date!

One farm boy got desperate, so he tried the blind date service. Not to say his date was ugly, but he found himself sitting at a bar, taking a shot of whiskey, looking in his pocket, taking a shot of whiskey, looking in his pocket, taking a shot of whiskey, looking in his pocket.

Finally, the bartender, getting annoyed (like you guys reading this), came over, asking what was going on.

"Well, my date is up in my bed waiting for me."

"Then why are you down here taking a shot of whiskey and looking in your pocket?"

"I got her picture in here, and when she looks good enough, I am heading up."

The bartender took one look and handed him the whole bottle! (I think she was a University of Michigan cheerleader.)

Farm Boy Gets One Up!

Farm boy takes a golfing gorilla to the local high-society country club and is told he can't golf there. He says, "I'm here to challenge your best golfer to a match for five thousand dollars."

The club pro, very cocky, comes over and says, "That would be me. Is the gorilla your caddy?"

"Oh no," says the farm boy. "I don't golf, the gorilla does!"

"The gorilla? You got to be kidding."

"You afraid to play him?" says the boy.

"Of course not, let's make it ten thousand."

"All right," says the farm boy.

The first hole is 400 yards par 4; the pro tees off first, driving 250 yards right down the middle, smiles, and says, "Your gorilla is up."

The gorilla drives the ball all the way to the green, and the pro can't believe it! Farm boy says, "I am surprised you haven't heard of the golfing gorilla. I feel bad. We could call it off for two thousand if you like."

Gladly, the pro gives him two thousand dollars. They go to the green to get the balls, and the pro says, "How does he putt?

Quote: "Just like he drives, four hundred yards!

(Way to go.)

One Tough Farm Boy!

Japanese farm boy joins the air force, ends up in the kamikaze unit; turns out he flew thirty successful missions! (I don't understand either; it's just what I heard.)

Farm Boy—Lucky or Not?

Farm boy going to town to see a friend and has car trouble right in front of a mansion. He goes up to the door, asking if he can stay the night because his car broke down. The recent widow said, "Sure, no problem." So in the door he goes.

They start drinking; one thing leads to another, and they end up in bed together. He doesn't want anybody to find out, so when she asks him his name, he gives his friend's name.

A few years later, his friend calls from the city and asks if he ever gave out his name.

"Yeah, I did. I'm sorry," says the farm boy.

"No problem," says the city boy. "A widow with no family died and left me her whole estate in the millions, leaving me a note thanking me for a wonderful night!"

(I say unlucky.)

Enterprising Farm Boy!

Billy just turned eighteen and had the house all alone for the first time all weekend. He decided to go to town and bring home a lady of the night (hooker). He had saved up to five hundred dollars, and that's just what the first one wanted for a night of pleasure.

"Great," said the farm boy, "but I got some strange stipulations." The lady said nothing was strange to her. Then she asked what they were. "I want to do it quietly and in total darkness."

"No problem. Let's go."

They got home, went up in his bed, did it once; he left, came back in, they did it again, and he left. By the sixth time, the lady goes, "Why, Billy, you seem to be getting stronger."

"Billy? I'm Sam. Billy's outside. He called up all his buddies promising them to see how a woman differs from a sheep for three hundred a pop. And frankly, I thought the sheep was better!"

(Holy cow—or in this case, sheep!)

Every Farm Boy's Dream?

Farmer returning from a trip hears at the coffee shop (where else?) that a neighbor's eighteen-year-old boy has been with every lady on the block (that's only three out in the sticks) but his wife. He wonders if it is true, so he asks his wife if that boy has been with all the neighbor's women but her; she starts crying, saying yes.

"That's good, isn't it?" says the farmer.

"No," she snaps, "he didn't even ask me." Still crying, she said, "He must think I'm ugly too!"

(He better be quiet.)

Like Father, Like Son, and Others!

The seventeen-year-old farm boy has had a crush all school year on the shy (so he thought) French exchange student at the neighbor's, a very good-looking young lady. Finally, they start dating, and she invites him into her bedroom when everybody is gone. The farm boy gets in bed with her but can't perform (make love). She says, "It sure is something with you Americans. My teacher, your dad, and my host parent have all had the same problem!"

(That's just wrong.)

Boys Are Boys, and Men Are Men!

An attractive blonde from Ireland came home with the farm boy from college. She seemed a little intoxicated but wanted to go with the farm boy and his dad to the men's poker night. The blonde got there and said, "I hope you don't mind, but I feel luckier completely nude."

As they dealt the cards, she discarded her clothes while putting all her money in the pot, yelling, "Come on, baby, mama needs new clothes and another ace." The well-endowed (big-boobed) Irish gal started jumping up and down, yelling, "I won, I won" as she threw in her cards, hugging each player. Then she picked up her clothes and quickly departed with all their money!

The farmers stared at each other dumbfounded (with a smile on); finally, one of them asked, "What did she have for cards."

The other answered, "Beats me. I thought you checked!"

Moral to the story: Not all blondes are dumb, not all Irish are drunks, but men are men (boys are boys, in the country or city!)

Even a Generation Ago, Farmers Got Mixed Up Too!

Back in the late '50s, a nice boy showed up to take the farmer's daughter out, but she wasn't ready (what a surprise). So they sat down to talk.

The dad asked, "You're the pastor's boy, aren't you?"

"Yes, I am," was the reply.

"Well, let me tell you. My daughter sure likes to screw."

"What?" the boy says.

"Yeah, she likes to screw and screw and screw."

"No kidding," said the boy, now with a big smile.

The dad says, "What are you guys going to do tonight?"

Boy says, "That sure changes my plans."

The daughter comes down, and the boy hustles her out to the car, smiling all the way. Few minutes later, the daughter comes in, crying, "It's the twist, the twist for the third time, Dad!"

(Ruined that boy's night.)

Farmers Are Farmers

Three women of the night (hookers) were discussing the men they liked sitting around at the bar. The first said, "I like priests."

"Priests?" the other two said. "Why them?"

She says, "Because they even bless you when you're done."

The second lady stated she really liked businessmen and businesswomen (don't want to be sexist) because they were always kind, businesslike, and good tippers.

The third says, "I don't know who my favorite client is, but I can tell you one group that I will stay away from." They ask her who that was. "Farmers," she stated.

One spoke up: "They seem real nice, I worked the Louisville farm show, and they treated me real nice."

"Not the ones I had. It was either too wet, too dry, or they want to pay me after fall, and that was *if* they got a good crop."

(Wives, now you know why your husband comes home from the farm shows smiling! Just kidding, maybe.)

Old School vs. New School

Good old country school just a few years ago versus new city school!

Scene 1:
OLD: Billy goes deer hunting before school and then pulls into the school lot with his shotgun in the gun rack. The principal, seeing this, goes to get his gun to show Billy!
NEW: School goes into lockdown. FBI is called. Billy goes to jail, never sees truck or gun again! Counselors are called in for traumatized teachers and students!

Scene 2:
OLD: Billy and Fred get into a fight after school in the playground. Crowd gathers. Billy wins. They shake hands and become best friends.
NEW: Police and SWAT come and arrest Billy and Fred. Both are expelled and go to jail even though Fred started it!

Scene 3:
OLD: Johnny will not be still in class and disrupts other kids, so he is sent to the office for a good paddling and never causes a problem again.
NEW: Johnny is given a huge dose of Ritalin, spaces out like a zombie,

and is said to have ADHD. The school gets extra money for his disability!

Scene 4:
OLD: Mark has a headache, takes an aspirin, and shares one with a teacher.
NEW: The police are called. Mark is expelled from school. His car, his locker, and his bedroom at home are all searched for drugs and weapons.

Scene 5:
OLD: Pedro fails English, goes to summer school, then to college, and becomes a policeman.
NEW: ACLU finds out, claims it's racist to require English. Pedro's English teacher is fired, and English is dropped as a requirement. Pedro is given his diploma anyway, but ends up a dishwasher because he can't speak English.

Scene 6:
OLD: Billy falls at school, scrapes his knee, and is found crying by his teacher. She hugs him, and in a short time, Billy is back playing.
NEW: The teacher is seen hugging the kid and fired, labeled a sexual predator. Billy undergoes five years of therapy at taxpayers' expense.

(Oh, for the good old country school!)

Farmers Like to Golf

Two farmers, Ralph and Leroy, went golfing every Tuesday no matter what! One Tuesday, they were on the green by the road. Ralph got ready to putt, but stopped, bent over, and tipped his hat to a funeral procession till it passed.
Leroy said, "You are such a gentleman, Ralph."
"Well, that was the *least* I could do for my wife!" (Very least!)

* * *

Ralph and Leroy were golfing and hit way out of bounds. Being farmers, they weren't going to lose new balls (they found them in the pond), so they went out and found them. Ralph, even though he was out of bounds, decided to play it where it was—in a patch of buttercups. He did and tore up a patch of them, causing Mother Nature to appear, yelling at him, saying he could no longer have butter for tearing up those buttercups.

Ralph, terrified, saw that Leroy had found his ball and was about to swing. He yells, "Stop, stop!" because Leroy was in a patch of pussy willows. (Close call.)

* * *

This time, four farmers—Ralph and Leroy were joined by Sam and George on their golf outing. They all teed off. George hit his way out of bounds. He stated that it was a new ball, so he was going to find it (a farmer).

The other three got to talking about how their sons were doing with the fifteen minutes they had! Ralph stated his was doing so good selling cars he even gave a friend a car.

Leroy says, "What a coincidence. Mine is doing so good selling jewelry he told me he gave a friend a five-thousand-dollar watch."

Sam says, "That's really strange. My son, who's in the investment field, told me he just gave a friend a ten-thousand-dollar portfolio."

George finally comes back and proudly states he found five balls.

"Hey, we were talking about our sons. How is yours doing?"

"Not good," said George, "and I don't want to talk about it." He seemed down the rest of the round.

Finally, one of them said, "We're all friends, tell us what is bothering you about your son."

"He came out of the closet."

"What's that?" they asked. "He gay."

"Oh," they all said. "That would be terrible. Does he seem to be doing OK?"

"Yeah," replied George. "One friend gave him a car, another a watch, and one even gave him a ten-thousand-dollar investment portfolio."

(Then the others were quiet!) E-mail if you have a good golf story.

There are a couple of more good golf stories I know, but I never wrote them down, and so far I can't remember them. (Must be old age.)

Farmer Messes Up—Literally!

One farmer working on the entertainment for the upcoming young farmers' banquet at the local VFW decided the budget was too tight to hire anybody. He fatefully comes up with the idea that he would be the entertainment. The young farmer read books, took an Internet course on hypnotism, and thought it would be great fun. The night of the banquet came; he felt ready and got up to do his routine. He was waving his watch, doing everything by the book; he didn't think it was working till he dropped his watch.

It broke all over the floor (he was mad since it cost him ten bucks at Walmart); without thinking, he yelled, "*Oh shit!*" And it took them two weeks to clean the hall up!
(This is the original dirty job.)

Backwoods Rural Divorce

Farmer who almost never came to town went to town to find a lawyer. He found a lawyer's office, went in, told them he wanted a divorce.
The lawyer said, "You want a divorce?"
"Yeah, one of them."
"Do you have grounds?"
"Yeah, thirty acres out yonder."
"No, no. I mean, do you have a case?"
"No, but I have a John Deere in the fence row."
The lawyer, really starting to get confused, was trying to think what to ask this good old boy, when he comes up with, "Is she a nagger?"
"Now," says the farmer, "you're gettin' somewhere. She sure isn't, but the new baby sure is!"

(Good luck, lawyer.)

Enterprising Farmer

Finally, after years of being nagged, the old farmer gave in to his wife's wishes to build a bathroom and do away with the outhouse. He was getting ready to tear it down when a lightbulb went off in his head. His neighbor went by, saw an antenna coming out of the outhouse, and stopped to see what was going on. The farmer explained that he put a bathroom in the house, came out to tear down the outhouse, but came up with the idea to rent it out!

The neighbor laughed and said, "Nobody will rent that."

Coming back a few weeks later, the neighbor saw two antennas coming out of the outhouse; in disbelief, he stopped to see what was going on. The farmer explained he had so many requests to rent it, he decided to rent the basement too! (Goodness gracious!)

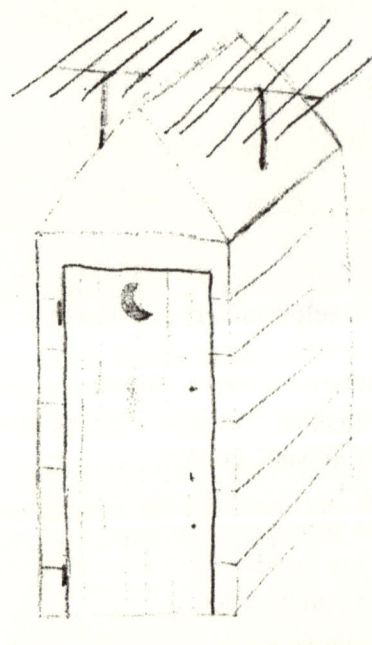

Another dream shattered!

Finally, someone has managed to photograph the pot at the end of the rainbow! Wouldn't you know it!

Wife Has Problems!

Farmer goes to the doctor, tells him he is worried about his wife's hearing because she wouldn't respond to him till he gets close to her.

The doctor says, "Let's see how close. Tonight at supper, when she is cooking, start at thirty feet. Ask what's for supper, keep moving in till she responds."

So that night, the farmer starts at thirty feet, asks what's for supper. No response. So he moves in to twenty feet, asks again. No response. Farmer moves in to ten feet and again asks, "What's for supper, honey?"

Finally, she turns around and yells, "Chicken, for the third time, you old fart!"

(Who needs the hearing aid?)

Wife Has Problems Again!

Same farmer at the doctor again says, "I'm worried about my wife." "Why this time?" replies the doctor, not too sure after the last ordeal.

"Well, when we have relations [make love], she's cold one time, the next she will be hot and clammy."

Doctor thinks a little and says, "I will talk to her about it." So the farmer goes out, and his wife enters the office. "Your husband is worried about you," says the doctor. "He said one time you make love, you're cold. The next time, hot, clammy."

"That old fart," says the wife. "It's because the first is in the winter, the second is in the summer, and I am hot and clammy because he is too damn cheap to buy AC!"

(*Again, who has the problem?*)

Farmer One-Ups Lawyer

A farmer named Billy had a pickup trailer accident. The trucking company's fancy lawyer is questioning Billy at the accident. "You said, 'I'm fine.'"

Billy says, "Well, I'll tell you what happened. I just loaded my favorite ass, Clyde, into the—"

"I don't want details," the lawyer interrupts. "Just answer me. Did you say, 'I'm fine' at the accident?"

Billy says, "I just got Clyde loaded, and I was driving when—"

The lawyer interrupts again. "Judge, I am trying to show this man told the policeman on the scene he was just fine. Now several weeks later, he is trying to sue my client, it's fraud."

By this time, the judge told the lawyer, "I'd like to hear about his favorite donkey, Clyde."

"Thank you," says Billy. "As I was saying, I just loaded Clyde, my favorite ass—"

Judge says, "I would prefer in court you use 'donkey.'"

"Sorry," says Billy. "I loaded my former ass, now donkey, Clyde, into my trailer and was driving down the highway when this gigantic semi-truck came out of nowhere and rammed my pickup right in the side. I was thrown into one ditch. Clyde was thrown into the other. I was hurting real bad and didn't want to move. Poor old Clyde was moaning and groaning, so I knew she was in bad shape by his moans. Right after the accident, a policeman came along and could hear Clyde moaning and groaning, so he went over to see her. Took one look at her condition and shot her right between the eyes. Then the policeman came over to me with the gun in his hand and asked me, 'How are you feeling?' Now, what, Mister Lawyer, would you say?"

(Gotcha!)

Old Farmers Talking

Three old farmers are talking about getting old. First farmer says, "I had an oil can in my hand but couldn't remember what I was going to oil."

The second farmer says, "I know what you mean. The other day, I was standing at the barn door and didn't know if I was coming or going."

The third old farmer pipes in, "Glad I'm not senile like you guys, knock on wood." Then he raps his knuckles on his wood bench and says, "Hey, somebody must be at the door. I will go get it!"

(Who's senile?)

Farmer Tries Hand at Inventing

He tried to turn in his invention under "Electric Bill Organizer" but got turned down. Note said his invention was already patented under "Paper Shredder."

(I think he was in financial trouble.)

* * *

The tough old farmer was telling us kids (I guess he thought we weren't tough enough) how he only felt pain twice in his life. "When was that?" we asked.

"Well, I was out west, bear hunting, and stepped on a bear trap. It snapped shut right between my legs."

"Ouch!" we all said. "When was the second time?"

Quote: "When I hit the end of the chain."

(*Ouch!*) *No picture needed*!

Farmer and Wife One-Ups FBI

Farmer and his wife get to reminiscing about the old schoolhouse getting ready to be razed (torn down). It was where they first had eyes for each other in third grade. They decided to walk down to see the old school before it was destroyed and their memories were gone. Into their old third-grade classroom they go, and sure enough, he finds the old desk where he carved his future wife's name.

All happy, they started heading home. As they walked, a Brink's truck goes by with the back door flinging open, and a big bag of money falls out. Against the farmer's better judgment, the wife wants to keep the large bag of hundred-dollar bills, so he takes it home and hides it in the attic. The next day, the FBI shows up, asking them if they have seen or heard about the money.

The farmer says, "I got it—"

His wife interrupts, stating that her husband is senile.

FBI states, "I would like to hear your husband's story anyway."

"Well," says the farmer, "it all started on the way home from school."

"That's it," says the FBI. "We're out of here. This is a waste of time. He's nuttier than a fruitcake."

(Who got who?)

Farmer's Daughter (Blonde)

Farmer's daughter is on her first trip away from the farm, and it is to Paris. She boards the plane, sits down in first class. The stewardess comes over, checks her ticket, then says it's for the back of the plane, in coach.

The farmer's daughter then says, "I am blonde, beautiful, and I'm going to Paris. I am sitting right here."

So the stewardess goes and gets the head stewardess. The head stewardess comes, explains, "That is not a first-class ticket, so you must move to the back."

Again the farmer's daughter says, "I am blonde, beautiful, and I'm going to Paris. I am sitting right here."

The stewardess, not knowing what to do, goes and gets the co-pilot. They explain the situation to him; he goes up, whispers in the blonde's ear. The blonde gets up and hustles to the back of the plane.

Puzzled, the stewardess goes up to the co-pilot and asks, "What did you tell her?"

Quote: "First class isn't going to Paris, just coach in the back!"

(Hope that's not your daughter.)

* * *

Same blonde is on the way home from Paris (yes, she did make it to Paris, thanks to that thoughtful co-pilot). The pilot comes on, says, "Don't worry, but we lost one motor, there's three left. It will delay us one hour."

Again the pilot comes on, saying, "Folks we lost a second motor. We're fine, we got two left, but this will delay us another hour."

The pilot is back again, saying, "We just lost the third motor, but we will make it, just three hours late though."

The blonde is really looking upset, and the guy beside her says, "Are you getting scared of crashing, like me?"

"No," says the blonde, "but if we lose one more motor, I'm afraid we will never get down!"

(Again, hope she's not your daughter.)

* * *

This good-looking blonde farmer's daughter was maybe a little stuck on herself. She was in a wreck, and they asked her for her vital stats. Quote: "Thirty-six, twenty-six, thirty-six!"

(OK, and I mean OK.)

* * *

I think this blonde farmer's daughter was just a little naïve. When she found out she was pregnant, she swore up and down it wasn't hers!

(She must have thought she was the farmer's boy!)

* * *

The next farmer's daughter had a goal to join a cult, and she talked her city boyfriend into joining with her. (Who's the dumb one here?) They found one and went to meet with the pastor, and he told them to join the cult, they had to restrain from relations (sex) for six months! The boyfriend, against his better judgment, agreed with his girlfriend to go ahead.

Three months in, they met with the pastor. He asked them if they stuck with the rules, and they said, "No problem." (At least she thought no problem). Fifth month, they again met with the pastor, saying that everything was going good, and they were following his orders to a tee. Finally, six months passed, so they went in to see the pastor; and he said, "Did you obey and ready to join the cult?"

The boyfriend said, "Pastor, I can't lie. We were doing fine till she dropped the soap a couple of days ago, bending over in front of me, and I couldn't control myself."

"Well, son, good of you not to lie. But you know the rules, so you can't be allowed in our church."

"That's OK," the boy said. "They won't allow us back in Kroger's either!"

(My, my, my.)

* * *

Farmer's wife was leaving for the day and told her blonde daughter to put the puzzle on the kitchen table together so she could frame it. When she comes home, she says to her daughter, "What have you been doing all day? I forgot to put the puzzle on the table."

"Oh no, you didn't," the daughter replied. "I've been working on it all day, but I can't get it to look like the tiger on the box!"

"You won't, that's the frosted flakes!"

(Further rocket scientist doesn't come to mind.)

* * *

Farm girl from a very strict family moves to town and gets a job at Hooters—just kidding. Actually, at the local hardware store, working at the counter. First day on the job, a rough construction worker from across the road comes and tells her he wants a bastard file. She gets upset and thinks he is using curse words at her, so she goes to get the manager.

The manager comes out and asks why the construction worker is using profane language with his help. The construction worker explains that he just asked for a bastard file. "Oh I'm sorry," the manager said and got the file. The manager explained to the farm girl, "That was a type of file, not profanity."

The next day, the farm girl's priest comes to see her, and he says he is working on a job that needs a file and he knows nothing about them. The girl wants to show how smart she is, tells him, "You need one of these bastards over here." The priest just looked down in disgust, muttering, "One day, and she is already talking like a city girl."

(By the way, Hooters is OK. I love their breasts. Ooops! I mean wings.)

* * *

Farmer's daughter (blonde, I think) went to the big city for the first time. She was starving, so she went to her first buffet, telling the waitress she wanted two. They seated her at a table for two. When the waitress came back, she said, "Where is the other person?"

The farmer's daughter said, "I'm here by myself."

The waitress said, "Then why did you order two?"

"Because I'm starving, duh!" (Duh duh!)

Farmer's Daughters Can Be Evil Too!

Farmer's daughter, a gorgeous blonde, went up to the bar in her small town. She gestured with a sexy whistle to the bartender, who approached her immediately. She seductively signaled that he should bring his face closer to hers. As he did, she gently caressed his full beard. "Are you the manager?" still stroking with both hands.

"Sorry, no," he said.

"Is he available? I need to speak to him," she asked as she ran her hands behind his beard and through his hair.

"I'm afraid he's not. Can I help you?"

"Sure, leave him a message." She ran her fingers across the bartender's lips and slyly popped a couple of her fingers in his mouth, allowing him to suck them gently.

Finally, the bartender, breathing very hard, managed to tell her, "What should I tell him?"

"Tell him," she softly whispers, "there is no toilet paper, hand soap, or even towels in the ladies' room, and that's really bad when it's that time!"

(Gee whiz!)

* * *

Farmer's daughter, blonde (*believe it or not*), was allergic to bees. She went to the doctor's office, telling him she got stung golfing. As he got ready to examine her, he asked where she was stung. Blonde: "By the bush, between hole one and two!"

(No comment.)

* * *

What's the first thing a farmer's blonde sixteen-year-old (thirteen in West Virginia) daughter does when she gets up in the morning? (Goes home.)

What do turtles and blondes have in common? Get them on their back, and they're both scr—. (Sorry, can't finish that one and keep the book PG.) Hint: the rest of the letters are e-w-e-d.

* * *

Young farm boy walks into the bar for the first time (which is at fourteen in West Virginia). Puzzled, he walks up to the bartender and asks what that hot blonde meant by saying she was drunk. The bartender says, "You got a lot to learn, that's her mating call."

The boy then asks, "What did the brunette over there mean by, 'Is the damn blonde gone yet?'"

"Well, sonny, that's her mating call!"

* * *

What does a farmer's smart blonde daughter, a happy farmer, and a kind-hearted lawyer have in common? Nothing; they don't exist.

(I better not say any more.) E-mail me with your best blonde joke.

Michigan University Jokes
Since we're all Ohio State fans

Do you know how to get a U of M grad off your porch?
(Pay for the pizza.)

A local farm boy got a date with a Michigan cheerleader; we asked him if he got her in his room. He said, "I got her to my doorway, and soon seen sweet talk wouldn't work, so I had to grease her hips and push like hell!

One boy, a grad of U of M, said, "We just used to turn them sideways."

"You would've seen her rear end, you would know why I couldn't!"

* * *

Do you know why they had to put Astro Turf down on the Michigan football field?
To keep the cheerleaders from grazing!

Do you know what you get when you cross a Michigan cheerleader with a pig?
Don't know; there are some things even a pig won't do!

Do you know how a Michigan cheerleader turns on the light after a night of making love?
Opens the car door!

Do you know where a Michigan football player goes when he wants a date?

Family reunion!

* * *

Another boy gets a date with a U of M cheerleader. He walks her out to the car, she gets in the front seat, and he says, "Hold on. I got to run back in the house."

Well, she really belches (a juicy one at that); she doesn't want him to smell it on her breath, so she gets a breath mint out. Then she raises her leg and rips a fart; she doesn't want him to smell that, so she rolls down the window and starts fanning it out. Finally, she sees he isn't coming yet, so she starts digging a booger out of her noise and quits five minutes later when she sees him coming.

He opens the door and says, "By the way, did you meet the couple we are double-dating with in the backseat?"

* * *

Do you know why the Michigan coach is only dressing twenty players for this year's big Ohio State game?

He is hoping the rest can dress themselves!

Do you know what Michigan football players do with their cheerleaders to celebrate a victory over Ohio State?

Nobody remembers that long ago!

E-mail me with your best U of M jokes or OSU or whoever you tell them about.

Farmer Gets Bride from the City

Farmer gets bride from the city (or farmersonly.com); anyway, he brings her home to the farm.

Just a few weeks after she is there, he has to leave for the day. He calls after he leaves, telling her, "The university doctor is coming, and I forgot to put a nail behind the cow he was to inseminate."

She says, "What?"

Farmer says, "To make big Bertha pregnant. You know which one she is, so go put a spike behind that stall."

"OK," she replies.

Then some girlfriends come from the city, and the wife says, "Come on, we're going to the barn."

They say, "What do you got to do?"

She says, "Somebody is coming, and I got to put a nail in the wall behind a certain cow."

"Why?" they ask.

The new bride: "I don't really know. I guess to hang his pants on!"

(Yee-ha!

* * *

Some rural communities get uptight about city people coming to the country. Take for example the bus of city tourists that ran off a country road into the quarry, and they all drowned. I read the newspaper the next day. Headline was, crying shame. I thought it was for the people that drowned. Nope. Turns out when they pulled up the bus, it had *one empty seat*!

(Good start, though. Just kidding.)

* * *

Tip: Quit looking at all your e-mails or you will...

- no longer open a public door without using a paper towel or have them put lemon slices in your ice water because of the bacteria on the peel!
- no longer use the remote in a hotel room because of what the last person did flipping through the adult movies!
- no longer sit down on hotel bedsheets. God only knows when they were last washed. (You can also thank *60 Minutes* blue light on this too!)
- no longer shake hands with a person driving a car since the number one pastime while driving is picking your noise, though cell phone usage is coming on fast. (No kidding!)
- no longer eat snacks since hearing about what the trans-fat will do!
- no longer have any savings after seeing that sick girl in Ethiopia and sending her all your savings! (Same one I later saw in Uganda.)
- no longer eat at KFC after seeing the conditions their chickens are raised in!
- no longer use deodorants because they cause cancer, so you will smell like your hogs! (But not as bad as my neighbor's wife, though.)
- no longer drive your car because of its carbon footprint and who owns the companies (Citgo owned by Venezuela, BP by Brits, and others).
- no longer drink beer since the last American brewer, Budweiser, is now foreign owned. (What am I saying? Forget this one!)
- no longer buy John Deere equipment.(Just because.) Hint: I sell Massey Ferguson.

Just don't believe everything you read on the Internet!

* * *

You probably farm in northern Ohio...

- if your local ice cream parlor closes from September to May! (My sister closes from October to April at her place in Carey, Ohio.)
- if someone in Lowe's offers you assistance, and they don't work there! (I am just glad to get assistance.)

- if you wear shorts and a coat at the same time! (I do all the time.)
- if you have long telephone conversations with somebody who dialed a wrong number (and you have severe problems)!
- if your yearly vacation is going just south of Columbus (and you'd be a cheap country hick)!
- if you have hit a deer twice in the same day!
- if you switched from heat to AC and back on the same day.
- if you carry jumper cables in your car and stopped to help somebody with them, and you don't even know them!
- if your kids' Halloween costumes fit over a snowsuit!
- if driving is better in the winter because the potholes are filled with snow. (Believe me, this is very true; you need to ride with me on some sales calls sometime.)
- if your road construction begins in March and ends in November! (Tip: invest in the company that makes the orange barrels.)
- if zero is OK as long as the wind isn't blowing! (You may need your head examined.)

E-mail me with any more.

* * *

Farmers, in most cases, are more honest than their city counterpart. Take the city slicker and the farmer killed in a car wreck. They're standing at the pearly gates (heaven), and Saint Pete lets them in, taking them into a big room full of clocks.

They ask, "What is this all about?"

Saint Pete says, "Well, when you sin, your clock goes ahead one minute."

The farmer asks, "Where is mine?"

Saint Pete points over there, and it's ahead seventeen minutes; not bad at all.

City slicker then asks, "Where's mine?"

"In the boss' (God's) office," said Saint Pete.

With a very cocky smile, the city slicker replies, "Probably to show people what a good person's clock looks like."

"Oh no," says Saint Pete. "He was hot and needed a fan!"

(That's been told many ways.)

Union or Non-union—That Is the Question

Union man goes to Vegas, decides to check out houses of ill repute (whorehouses). He goes to the first place. "Is this a union house?"

"No."

"So what is the woman's cut on a hundred bucks?"

"Twenty," is the reply.

He goes to four more places, all the same answer. Finally, he sees a sign that says, "Union women work here." So he goes in, and sure enough, it is a union whorehouse.

The union man says, "What is the woman's pay on a hundred bucks?"

"Eighty," replies the madam.

"Great," replies the union man. "I will take that gorgeous blonde over there."

"This is a union house, sir. Ethel over there has first seniority."

"Oh my lord, how old is she?"

"Don't know, we lost track at one hundred!"

(Good lord.)

Even Farmers Get Old!

Even farmers have problems we haven't considered yet! The ninety-year-old farmer was requested by his doctor for a sperm count as part of his physical exam.

"Take this jar home, bring it back with a sample tomorrow," said the doctor. The farmer came back in with the jar just as empty as the day before! "What happened?" asked the doctor.

The old farmer said, "Well, it was like this. I tried with my right, then my left hand. Nothing happened, so I got my wife to help. She tried with her right, then her left hand, then with her mouth, first with her teeth in, then with her teeth out. All this, still nothing! We got the neighbor to try too, first with both hands, then an armpit, and she even tried squeezing it between her knees, but still nothing."

The doctor was shocked. "You asked a neighbor?"

"Yep, and we still couldn't open that damn jar!"

(Wondered where this was going, didn't you?)

I read this somewhere years ago and decided that it was a good story to end on!

Finally! Farm Life vs. City Life

A father of a very wealthy, high-class family from the big city took his son on a trip to the country. He wanted to show how poor the people in the country were so his son would appreciate what their family had. They spent a couple of days at the place of a cousin the father considered very poor. When they got home, he asked the son how he liked the trip.

"Great," replied the boy.

"Do you now see how the very poor live?" asked the father.

"Sure do."

"And what did you learn from this?"

"Well," the boy said, "we got one dog, they have three! Our pool is big, but their creek has no end! We have imported lanterns in our yard, but they have the stars at night! Our lot is big for town, but their lot is endless! We have servants who serve us, but they serve each other! We have walls and security cameras protecting us, their friends and neighbors protect them."

The father didn't know what to say.

The boy added, "Thanks, Dad, for showing me how poor we really are!"

In all seriousness, I have been poking fun at myself and rural America, but I don't think any of us would trade this wonderful life!

Chapter 4

Cheap Country Hick

This is a new segment I'm introducing called "Cheap Country Hick (CCH)."

You could be one...

1. if you turn your underwear inside out to get one more day and save on laundry detergent.
2. if three days later you're still putting layers of coffee over the old in the maker to save a three-cent filter!
3. if you wait for the toilet to really need flushing (brown) to save on your water bill (you're one)!
4. if you keep the good hot dogs to yourself while giving the kids the crappy ones to save on your food bill! (Ask my wife about this.)
5. if you rotate your bald tires to get another one hundred miles! (You're a CCH, and a dangerous one at that.)
6. if you climb the TV tower to change the direction of your antenna to save on electricity! (Don't ask my wife about this one.) Actually, it was because I was too cheap to fix the rotor motor.
7. if you go to every farm-equipment and truck dealer's open house asking for a take-home bag!
8. if you wash plastic spoons and paper plates to save from buying a ninety-nine-cent pack! (I got a family member that does this one.)

9. if you reuse plastic baggies to save a nickel!
10. if you go to all the local fairs to get all the freebies and then trade with your neighbors!
11. if you only buy what you got coupons for at the grocery to save ten cents (whether you need it or not)!
12. if you only go to your favorite restaurant on your birthday—for the free dessert!
13. if you only go to your favorite bar on the second Tuesday of the month for two-for-one drinks! (And it's between six and seven in the morning!)
14. if you recycle everything, including the kids' bathwater, two for the price of one! (Hope first one didn't pee!)
15. if you unplug everything, including the clock, when you go away to save one dollar in electricity! (And you don't know how to reset the clock.)
16. if you have Christmas on the twenty-eighth so you can buy the gifts on the twenty-sixth for half price. (Darn good idea too!)
17. if you test-drive a pickup truck (1987or 1988) to impress your in-laws when they come over and return it when they leave. (Tip: Don't forget to change the plates.)
18. if your entertainment budget is to go out after a storm and drive around to see whose trailer blew away! (Great fun, by the way.)
19. if you make two dollars change in the church offering plate! (Hope it's not for the strip club!)
20. if your fifth child is wearing your first's clothes, and one was a girl, and the other a boy.
21. if you spend more than ten minutes looking for a golf ball because it was the first time you hit it! (After finding it in the water.)
22. if your sewer pipe goes straight to the creek because you're too cheap to buy a permit for a septic system! (Trust me, there is a lot of this going on.)
23. if you reuse wooden toothpicks to save one cent! (And it's not even yours!)
24. if you make your wife buy off the dollar menu on her birthday. You're one cheap CCH! (And you won't be busy when you get home.)
25. if you use your Leatherman (probably an imitation) to pull a tooth to save on a dentist bill!
26. if you're forty and still living at home. (Guess what you are.)
27. if you run coax from your mom's satellite dish five hundred yards away (then need to call her collect to change channels).

28. if you married your first cousin to save on wedding invitations! (Because both sides would be the same. Duh duh!)
29. if you get married in your backyard and have the mayor (uncle) to do the ceremony! (To save $25 on the church rental and $25 on the pastor (not quite $25 on the pastor since you had to buy your uncle a case of Busch beer). Guess where my daughter's was held?
30. if your honeymoon is to your local double-A baseball park for free on ladies' night! (You might be sleeping by yourself too!)
31. if you take all the ketchup packs off your table, then send the kids to the other tables to keep from buying a ninety-nine-cent bottle of ketchup for home! (I can relate to this one too!)
32. if you reuse sanitary products to save a buck! (You're a CCH, and a gross one at that.)
33. if you bring your pickup up behind a semi on the interstate (at 75 mph) to draft and save fuel! (And you insist it only works if you're within five feet!)
34. If you go to garage sales to save a buck on a wedding gift or your kid's birthday! (Sounds good to me, if I could get my wife on board.)
35. if your idea of taking your wife to a smorgasbord is the free samples at Sam's Club while she shops; you're a charter member!
36. if you messed around with your neighbor's wife because it was close, and you saved on fuel. (Forgot it was your sister though.) At least it wasn't your mother!
37. if you keep the mud on the truck till Thursday, fifty-cent-off day at the car wash! (Personally, I would wait till the cheerleader fundraiser!) Just kidding, Lori.
38. if you wait for three or more cows to get sick so you only get to pay the vet for one farm call! (You're a CCH, and a cruel one at that.)
39. if you find uses for used motor oil to save on disposal fee. Or do like most farmers—pour on the ground. (Sounds like a good topic for another book—"101 Uses of Used Motor Oil.")
40. if you look for a new pickup in the "$2,000 and Under" section.
41. if you tell the kids there is no Easter bunny so you don't have to buy eggs! (And they're only three and four!)
42. if you combine your anniversary and the kids' birthdays to save on cakes! (And they're three months apart!) We only stretch it two months.

If you can relate to these or know any good ones, e-mail me.

I'm not afraid to tell you I could relate to a lot of these and enjoyed coming up with them!

Now ready to take the CCH test? Just go back; see how many you have done or could possibly relate to!

SCORE

5 or less	Fortune 500 person
6-15	Normal cheap
16-20	Very cheap
21 or more	Congratulations! You're a Cheap Country Hick. Your author scored a 27!

Closing

In closing I really want to thank the American farmers, without them our business (Schmidt Machine), my travels or this book would not have been possible. Long live the American farmer, the family farm and the rural way of life!

I hope you understand this is a lighthearted book meant to bring humor to your life in these trying times and also to show there is real humor in rural America. Please e-mail me with your ideas, stories, or jokes I could use for another book or stand-up comedy show. I would like to know what you liked or disliked about this book and what I could have done better.

God bless! Remember, it's easy to find fault and problems, but dig deep to find humor in everything you do!

Remember Schmidt Comedy. "It's full of it."
cheapcountryhick@aol.com

Author's disclaimer

While you may lose weight reading this book
(by laughing your rear end off), it is not a proven
weight loss book.
>   Thank you,
>   Kevin

I have seen Kevin in action. These stories are
true and very funny—even strange.
Somewhat warped, little bizarre, but well worth reading.
>   —Rick Riggs
>   (Hazardous material mover, Linde Corp., Murray Hill, NJ)

Kevin brings out great humor between city
and rural life, and I have seen him on stage in
his comedy act. He is a country hick.
>   —Lynn Oldham
>   (A real rural American farmer, Rural USA)

Don't forget to take the cheap country hick (C.C.H.) test at the end of the book (e-mail me the results).

www.ingramcontent.com/pod-product-compliance
Lightning Source LLC
Chambersburg PA
CBHW021015090426
42738CB00007B/791